IS
NETWORKING
FOR
YOU?

A
Working Woman's
Alternative
to the
Old Boy System

Barbara B. Stern, Ph.D.

A SPECTRUM BOOK

Prentice-Hall, Inc. Englewood Cliffs, New Jersey 07632

Library of Congress Cataloging in Publication Data

Stern, Barbara B
Is Networking For You?

  (A Spectrum Book)
  Includes index.
    1. Women executives.   2. Women's networks.   I. Title.
HF5500.2.S698   650.1'3'024042   80-25225
ISBN 0-13-505966-6
ISBN 0-13-505958-5 (pbk.)

To H.S., The Transition Man

Prentice-Hall International, Inc., *London*
Prentice-Hall of Australia Pty. Limited, *Sydney*
Prentice-Hall of Canada, Ltd., *Toronto*
Prentice-Hall of India Private Limited, *New Delhi*
Prentice-Hall of Japan, Inc., *Tokyo*
Prentice-Hall of Southeast Asia Pte. Ltd., *Singapore*
Whitehall Books Limited, *Wellington, New Zealand*

CONTENTS

01/12/81 - $12.95

PREFACE

This book is in your hands today because of a process I call *networking*.

One day I had lunch with my stockbroker, a woman account executive, to discuss my purchase of municipal bonds. Within ten minutes, we agreed on the best "munie" to buy, and the sale was made. That was the most significant $5000 I ever spent. Our discussion quickly turned from bonds to the need for women in Bergen County, New Jersey, to meet each other on a professional level, much as men do in Rotary clubs. My broker, long denied admission to Rotary (even today, except in California, women must be Rotariannes or Rotariettes, or some such nonsense) articulated a desire for a similar women's group: a group of professional women, from all areas of business and the academic world, who could get together on a regular basis. Such a group would benefit women isolated within their own areas of expertise: yes, women lawyers did talk to other women, but mostly they were other women lawyers in the various Women's Bar Association groups. Both my broker and I agreed that it would be useful for women lawyers to talk to women dentists, and women dentists to women engineers, and so forth.

We decided to form a *network* group in Bergen County and to meet once a month for a long lunch. Our philosophy was that any woman who could not or would not spare two hours for lunch—even if she had to take a cut in pay for the purpose—would not be eligible. We would invite a cross section of women from the business, professional, and academic worlds. Subsequently we met with two women lawyers who had formed the third all-woman partnership in the county, and the four of us set up a nucleus of what would eventually be a full-fledged network of Bergen County's successful women. We each invited two or three successful women we knew and liked to the first luncheon: the group of fourteen women became the "founding mothers."

From this group, our own network has expanded to fifty members today. We have made many difficult decisions, including the selection of criteria for membership. We have received a tremendous amount of publicity, for, except in a few major cities where women are more advanced in organization, a group of successful women forming an organization for peer support is indeed newsworthy. The "news" is that we are here, and we have decided to team up for our personal benefit and for the benefit of society as well. The headlines have finally made the *Business* section, rather than the *Fashion* section of the newspaper; they reflect awe and some apprehension at the prospect of successful women uniting rather than competing.

Networking can benefit every professional woman. Let me give you an example of how it worked for me. As I mentioned earlier, this book is a product of networking. When I first decided to write a book on networking, I didn't know where to begin. I called Florence Donohue, an eminent tax attorney and one of our founding members, who worked in the tax department at Prentice-Hall. Florence was excited about the idea, presented it to other people at Prentice-Hall, and several hours later called me back with the name of the editor to contact in the Spectrum Books Division of Prentice-Hall.

I had networked! When I called Lynne Lumsden, the Senior editor of Spectrum Books, she told me to send in an outline, biographical information, marketing studies, and then asked me if I thought my book was really helpful — roughly translated as, "Would it sell?" My answer to her was as follows: "Networking works. If it were not for that process, I wouldn't be on the phone with you right now. We are networking!" The crucial name, the properly timed words of encouragement, and the professional contact took place because a tax attorney and an English professor happened to have lunch once a month in New Jersey. Networking works for women, often in unpredictable ways. This book suggests ways to create your own contacts with other professional women for the benefit of all.

Why NETWORK?

CHAPTER ONE

Imagine the following item in the *Business* section of the *New York Times:*

> *Jane Lawyer and Jeanette Manager were college*
> *roommates. Afterward they played tennis together*
> *regularly as Ms. Lawyer climbed the legal ladder and*
> *Ms. Manager progressed up the corporate organization*
> *chart. When Ms. Manager became chief executive*
> *officer of the XYZ Corporation, she retained Ms.*
> *Lawyer's law firm.* [1]

This item *was* in the *Business* section of the *New York Times;* the only difference was that the names were "John Lawyer and Joseph Manager," and the pronouns were

---

[1]"Business and the Law," by Tom Goldstein, June 22, 1979. ©1979 by The New York Times Company. Reprinted by permission:

"John Lawyer and Joseph Manager were college roommates. Afterward they played tennis together regularly as Mr. Lawyer climbed the legal ladder and Mr. Manager progressed up the corporate organization chart. When Mr. Manager became chief executive officer of the XYZ Corporation, he retained Mr. Lawyer's law firm."

masculine. The entire process of interwoven social, personal, and professional relationships—the *old boy NETWORK*—is summarized in that paragraph. And the key word is *boy*. Until recently, the process of *networking* has been a male activity, so automatic that it has not been deemed worthy of much analysis. There is probably more information on how to set up a football team than on how to set up a NETWORK. For this reason, the steps in networking have to be analyzed so that women can understand the process and begin to create their own "new woman networks." We have to start from square *A* in the networking game and provide a clear game plan for women to use. First we have to understand the game itself, its legitimacy, and its power.

THE NETWORKING FABLE

Let's look again at the the *Times* paragraph to see the kinds of relationships that cause men to associate in beneficial business ways. Remember, Mr. Lawyer and Mr. Manager eventually end up doing business, presumably to the advantage of both. First of all, the men were college roommates. This indicates, if not similar backgrounds, at least similar social status and, indeed, *some* social status. There are no dorms at Bronx Community College. The tennis partnership is a classic example of the locker room syndrome: the men obviously developed a personal relationship and associated regularly during nonbusiness hours in an informal atmosphere. This atmosphere may be permanently womanproofed. If every barrier between the sexes should disappear, I still foresee separate locker rooms and bathrooms in this country for many, many years. When the E.R.A. goes down in defeat because women fear unisex bathrooms, it seems unrealistic to expect coed locker rooms to form women's path to the old boy NETWORK. The informality of locker-room acquaintances, the shared social status of belonging to the same clubs, clearly carries over into business relationships for men.

The proof is that Mr. Manager and Mr. Lawyer did business together eventually; the social and personal connections paid off. To summarize (which is not breaking a butterfly on a wheel for a woman thinking this whole process over), Mr. Manager knew Mr. Lawyer through nonbusiness activities and then used him in business ways. Conversely, Mr. Lawyer used his social tie—his knowing Mr. Manager—to further his own business. There were other options: Mr. Manager could have sought bids from three law firms before hiring one; Mr. Lawyer could have investigated *XYZ* Corporation's Dun and Bradstreet rating, Annual Reports, and P & L Sheets before *he* signed on. Chances are neither man did anything of the sort; they simply networked.

WHO DO YOU KNOW?

In the process of gaining jobs, favors, or access to power, the basic principle of networking is, *Who do you know?* This appears to be a relatively easy principle to adapt for the new woman NETWORK. It's not. I had lunch recently with a woman assistant superintendant of schools in upper New York State. She is a quiet, cheerful, unabrasive woman, aware of her rights but unwilling to wreak havoc to get them. She told me a horrifying story of discrimination against her when she applied for a full superintendant position in another district; the discrimination was so blatant that a member of that district's Board of Education wrote to my friend suggesting that a case be brought before the State's Commission on Human Rights. My friend asked me whether I knew any lawyers who could advise her! I was astounded and asked, "Surely you must know a woman lawyer in your area who could tell you what to do?" She replied, "No. I don't know any women lawyers. Maybe there aren't any up here." After much probing, I discovered that my friend was on the same community service board as a woman legislator, the same college advisory board as a woman mayor, and the same charity board as a woman commissioner of education. But she didn't think she knew any women lawyers!

So the question, *Who do you know?* requires an examination of the concept, *to know*, as it applies to networking. Since networking is about the conscious efforts women must make to know each other, the many meanings and implications of the word must be examined.

The idea of knowing is obviously a loaded one, and a threatening one to women, yet the concept is crucial to networking. Women cannot form alliances, relationships, and contacts with other women until they become comfortable with the legitimacy of knowing them.

CARNAL KNOWLEDGE

One reason that women have had such tremendous difficulty with the idea of knowing other women is that the word is filled with sexual overtones. *To know* has long been synonymous with sexual knowledge. The biblical connotations of sexual knowledge have made *knowing* almost a dirty word in popular speech. This process has occurred with other words, such as *friend*, *relationship*, and all the other words used to define personal interactions in an age of disinvolvement. When a business leader says, "Sure, I know Mary," his meaning is in doubt until he adds, "She's the best operations research manager in the industry." Whether the business leader is male or female, the "Sure, I know Mary," frequently gives rise to an "Oh? How so, may I ask?" However, when Mr. Manager says, "Sure, I know John," no such questions arise. Mr. Manager will say, "He's been my tennis partner for years," and the conversation will proceed.

Women are reluctant to deal with the concept of knowing because it so often evokes a giggle or a dirty smirk when applied to women. At a political cocktail party, a woman accountant told a mixed audience that she was going to read the riot act to the president of the Board of Education about the recent drop in reading scores. The board's president is another woman, and the accountant said, "I think after all these years I know her well enough to tell her to watch her shop a little better." The audience reacted with suppressed laughter, raised eyebrows, and hints of sexual innuendos. The accountant continued, "After all, she is my sister."

INVISIBLE WOMEN

If women are not deterred from their efforts to know other women by the sexual implications of the word, they may be vanquished by their own insecurity. Women often think of themselves as invisible. If you are invisible, how can you know or be known? Even some very successful women are bedeviled by a lack of belief in their own visibility, and thus a firm conviction that they know no one at all. Considering this, it is a wonder that any two women get together to do business at all.

For a woman to feel that she knows another woman, she practically has to be her mother's best friend's daughter, her sorority sister, a next-door neighbor for ten years, or an upstanding member of her favorite charity and at least two other public service organizations. All that men need to do to know each other is to use adjacent urinals. The difficult admission, "I know her," has its roots in a female insecurity as old as time. Women, even the most successful ones, often think of themselves as invisible at best: they have no official stance, no professional posture, no office demeanor. One of the most successful women I have met, the marketing manager of a Fortune 500 company, develops agonizingly painful throat lesions before every convention. The medication she takes to soothe her throat enough for her to speak has a side effect: it causes skin blotches and redness. As a result, this normally attractive and easy-going woman is in pain, both physical and emotional, every year at convention time. When I asked her why she did not switch doctors or demand some other medication, she said, "Well, it doesn't make much difference. No one really sees me anyway." Such self-torture both to express invisibility and to reinforce it is, unfortunately, fairly common.

The roots of women's desire to pass unnoticed lie deep in history and psychology; the proof of this desire is the large numbers of women in specialized careers, functioning essentially as loners within corporate structures and in the professional and academic worlds.

Since women do not think of themselves as visible, they have great difficulty with the concept of knowing another woman well enough to make contact. It is extremely difficult for one woman to approach another in a professional sphere to ask a question, let alone a favor. This difficulty has prevented women from networking on the grounds that they cannot possibly know someone well enough to ask her to join a group.

ANATOMY IS DESTINY

When Freud wrote "Anatomy is destiny," he certainly did not have networking in mind, let alone the architecture of modern plumbing. While women need a long history of friendship to feel they know one another, a man will consider that he knows a man who uses the adjacent urinal. Men define knowing other men in a far looser, less intense, more practical way. Men feel perfectly free to announce that they know lockermates, clubmates, and tennis partners well enough to ask questions, opinions, favors, even free advice that women would never dream of requesting. In our beginning fable, Mr. Lawyer and Mr. Manager knew each other so well on the basis of college fraternizing and later tennis-playing that they unhesitatingly did business together, without any prior business knowledge of each other. Many men ask for, and get, physicals from doctor friends—the famous locker-room checkup—while women need six weeks of assertiveness training before they even request a consultation if they're uneasy about the family doctor's diagnosis. Men have traditionally felt free to garner information from even casual acquaintances, while women can barely stammer out legitimate requests for routine data from female peers.

Perhaps the rationale for such disparate definitions of knowing is the men's sure knowledge that *they have something to offer in return:* Mr. Lawyer and Mr. Manager have favors to trade, as do Mr. Doctor and Mr. Accountant. Free advice from a man you know isn't really free: it represents a debt to be paid off in kind in the future, a mafioso contract trading favor for favor. Men can afford to know each other and make use of casual acquaintances, secure in the knowledge that each will eventually end up in the other's office. The fraternity of man is a venerable, established club; the members know the rules. Since men expect to be in careers for life, they don't have to return the cup of sugar immediately; sooner or later their debts will come due. The vast and complex web of old boy networking is probably best explained to women by a Mafia analogy: men are making each other "offers they can't refuse." And as long as the offers are mutually beneficial, there is no stigma attached to the process. Mafia methods are the same as those of any organized institution, except that they are easier to understand. The nastiness lies in the ends, not in the means, and women can begin to NETWORK successfully when they separate legitimate uses of people they know from illegitimate manipulation and corruption.

YOU DON'T HAVE TO LOVE HIM . . .

The old saw passed down by every woman's mother, "You don't have to love him to go out with him," summarizes different male and female feelings about knowing others. Women have immense difficulty accepting the casualness of knowing without the need for great and prolonged intimacy. Women must separate deep friendship from business contacts before extensive networking can begin. The legitimacy of using casual acquaintances as a means of organizing for professional advancement is a new notion for women. All of the years outside men's rooms, locker rooms, and club rooms, have kept them from knowing the casual business relationships which are neither intimate, long-standing, nor even particularly personal, but are of such great value. All that is needed to form helpful business relationships is to have something in common—the same indefinable something men have in common when they join the same club, play tennis together, or shower in the same locker room.

Because women have been buried so completely in the sea of deep feelings, and because they have entered the career force so late and in such relatively small numbers, they must learn to appreciate the practical benefits of knowing many people in many (less intense) ways. Partly this involves the conscious development of unemotional ideas of knowing: women have to work towards casual, easy-going relationships which evolve in a cool, professional way. These relationships will never be devoid of human feeling; they will be, rather, detached from them. Of course a NETWORK can include women who become friends, women drawn together by force of personality, common interests, or sheer warmth. But networks can also include women acquaintances, drawn together by no other bond than the common need for career guidance, advice, and peer support.

This is illustrated in the kind of knowing that emerged between a commodities broker and a pediatric allergist, both members of a suburban woman's NETWORK. The women were quite opposite in personality: the broker was flamboyant, aggressive, hard-sell, proud to say that she had to make a hundred calls to sell one major lot of pork belly futures, triumphant in her ability to tolerate rejection. The doctor was shy, nearly inarticulate, protected almost totally from the adult world by her staff and her patients, and utterly unaccustomed to any form of assertive behavior. They regarded each other with suspicion but had enough in common in terms of education, social standing, and earning capacity to associate at NETWORK luncheons and meetings without ever making close contact. One Memorial Day weekend, the broker's son developed a frighteningly high fever, mysterious breathing difficulties, and a racking cough. The broker called her pediatrician; he was away, and an associate was on call. The associate saw the child and rendered an unsatisfactory diagnosis. When the child grew sicker, the broker took him to a nearby hospital, a small, non–teaching facility. While under treatment there, he grew even more desperately ill. The broker knew that she needed an expert. She called the shy pediatric allergist, who had the boy transferred to a major teaching hospital, ordered a tracheotomy performed, and then assembled a staff of experts to diagnose and treat him. The pediatrician saved the boy's life, not only by what she *did*, but also by who she *knew*. And the broker reached that pediatrician by *knowing* her in the useful, professional, contact-making way that is networking.

NETWORKING VS. KINGMAKING: THE USES OF POWER

Just as women have difficulty with the ideas implicit in *to know*, they shudder at the ideas contained in *to use*. Women feel an extraordinary distaste for using others and shrink from the very concept; they are repelled by accusations of manipulation. Although for centuries women have been kingmakers, powers behind the throne, influential only through others, still the accusation, "You're *using* her," causes discomfort. Now that women have decided to take power for themselves in legitimate and direct ways, they fear even the suspicion of manipulative behavior. Like reformed smokers who crusade against the vile weed, women who are— collectively—no longer kingmakers, but who hold power themselves, cannot accept the perfectly legitimate uses of connections.

The barriers between women achievers have been so great that only now are women beginning to learn what is legitimate reaching out and questioning, and what is unprofessional, gauche behavior. Women are just beginning to learn that they can use each other in mutually productive and supportive ways on the fast track to power. Women can now rule in their own right, and they can rely on other women as their allies. Women can help other women, provide support systems, and form peer groups without deceitful intent, manipulative behavior, or conniving motives. The word *use* has to be cleaned up in the same way the word *know* was, it is not wrong, dirty, or unfair to seek help from women who can help.

GET UNDRESSED, AND WE'LL SEE

There is a clear enough line between reasonable inquiry and unprofessional demands. The use of connections involves respectable ways women can help other women by means of career leads, emotional support, or both. A woman lawyer can surely ask a woman dentist a question about root canal, but it is not acceptable for the lawyer to thrust her open mouth into the dentist's face at a party. People who ask professionals for "free advice" go too far even when friendship is involved. All that professionals have to sell is their time, and undue infringements on it are not welcome. A doctor friend has the perfect solution to this kind of pushy use: whenever anyone at a party begins asking him complicated personal health questions, he whips out a stethoscope, puts on a look of grave concern, and says, "Get undressed right now, and we'll see what's wrong." But this doctor is unusual in that he pulls his routine on men as well as women! Most men seem to know the line between a reasonable question and an awkward, antisocial, amateurish demand. Even if men ignore this line, they still know it. This is the line that women are just starting to perceive, even as they are just learning how to contact other women professionals, how to ask legitimate questions, and what the questions *are*.

Since women in large numbers are relatively new to career positions, the process of legitimately using other women becomes a very deliberate and conscious exploration of the boundaries of the careers themselves as well as a networking activity. Most women do not know what they can ask other women even in their own area of specialization, without being thought dumb, pushy, or crafty. Because a measure of self-assertion is required even to ask a question, many women would rather remain silent and puzzled in lieu of asking what ultimately turns out to be obvious. A young lawyer told me that she suggested some very practical programs for her local Women's Bar Association: for example "How to Handle a Closing," "How to Write a Will," and many other practical matters not taught in law school. She was told by an older woman lawyer that when the older woman had suggested the same thing years ago, the best advice she got was to buy a legal secretary's handbook. The fledgling attorney would at least appear in the right court with the right papers on the right day! However, the young lawyer was determined, and she set up the programs to teach the younger women the skills their elders had acquired by painful and embarrassing trial and error.

If women within one field are only beginning to make use of other women as resources, imagine the difficulties in deciding how to approach women outside one's own area. My experience has been that the process of reaching out to other women is probably most comfortable when it begins *within* a single profession, industry, or corporation. The common bond of women working in the same field, as well as being on approximately the same power-money-status axis, does a great deal to encourage open exchange of ideas. Still, the process of sharing and using is very slow to grow. Even women lawyers, highly organized for over forty years, have to send out feelers and search each other out, because the whole idea of networking for support and advancement is so new. It may take months, or even years, for women meeting on a regular basis to feel comfortable enough with each other to ask, "Have you heard of any good openings in labor law?" or "What are some start-up costs in opening my own practice?" The hoped-for answer could be, "I know that XYZ's outfit needs a labor attorney; why don't you tell them I suggested you?" And so, networking within a profession gets going.

AN UNCOMMON GROUP

But networking outside one's own bailiwick, making use of women in different career areas, requires even more careful delineation of boundaries. The women who decide to group together on interdisciplinary lines soon find that each must articulate her own area of expertise, and clearly define what she does and how she does it, to enable her to use others and be properly used in return. The college dean has to explain her job functions carefully; she must describe her role in recruiting students, admitting them, running workshops for their benefit, analyzing transcripts, and preparing budgets. The owner of a graphics design firm must do the same; she has to explain that she creates the logo, oversees the copywriting, supervises the pictures taken and used, selects the colors and styles of paper and print, handles the layouts and mechanicals, and okays the final product. Only after these job descriptions are exchanged can the dean say, "What do you think of our catalog?" The design firm's owner may answer, "It's a workmanlike job, but I think it could be spiffed up a bit. You're selling to students, and the competition is tough." In this way, the beginnings of a possible business association are born; perhaps the dean will eventually insist that her friend be used for producing the next catalog.

This process of trading information is a learning process. Perhaps the most important function that networking provides is the opening-up of legitimate uses of another's skills. It is hardly possible for a group of different careerists, all relatively new to the working world, to understand what each other does. Every group of women is an uncommon group in that each has to explain her task to the others. A simple method of doing this, to be discussed further in later chapters, is the roundtable introduction: each woman gives her title, job description, and list of duties and responsibilities. This helps the women understand the skills available to them in the group, and see ways in which their own skills will have value to the others. For example, a woman doctor might say to a woman banker, "Well, you'd be the one to ask about all that literature I receive from the bank every month, trying to persuade me to switch to time deposits." When the banker responds, "Why don't you come in, and we'll analyze your cash flow to see whether that kind of money market account *is* best in your situation," the real networking seeds have sprouted.

Once the process of questioning and answering becomes demystified, and women start to learn what other women do, the whole matter of using each other becomes more acceptable as a sensible deployment of resources. Women have every reason to turn to other women for help and emotional support on the way up. This natural interchange has been blocked in the past by a hesitancy to get involved in what has been perceived as the negative side of the old boy NETWORK: the manipulative use of people by opportunists, the elevation of incompetents, the heavy sexuality implicit in knowing and using. Such negative expectations can be altered by experiencing the many benefits of cooperation and net-working.

SUMMARY

For too long women have feared being labeled manipulative if they requested information from someone, if not older, at least wiser. Women have feared laying claims to knowing anyone not related to or loved by them. They have feared that reaching out to one another would appear either pushy or dumb. All this is changing rapidly.

A woman personnel supervisor, in charge of EEO for an enormous health-care service facility, recently told me that a young man had asked an acquaintance of hers whether the EEO supervisor knew of any jobs in person-nel. The EEO woman said, "Let your friend come to my office and see me; I think there may be an opening in an entry-level slot, since the word is out that ABC is leaving. I am not really supposed to provide direct job leads, but I'd like to speak to the fellow and tell him how to go about this." Two days later the EEO supervisor called me in a fury: the young man had bypassed her completely. He had never come to see her, but instead went to the per-sonnel director and used her name. He used the old line, "Ms. EEO Supervisor suggested that I see you about an upcoming job." She told me, "I made sure that kid will never get his application looked at in this company! Can you imagine the nerve of this guy, using my name and deliberately going against my instructions!" I think we may have come full circle when women now accuse men of being manipulative, bitchy, and users of those in power.

But it is only in the very recent past that women have functioned in a climate where they could get to know and use each other effectively and responsibly. Women can now gain from each other in positive ways; they can overcome the barriers that have kept them apart for many years. The formation of networks enables women to know and use other women for professional support and personal reinforcement. The spontaneous formation all over the country of NETWORK groups is the strongest indication that women cooperating with women is an idea whose time is here. Networks recognize the old saw, "Knowledge is Power." When women combine to exchange knowledge, they create forums for sharing information. A significant element in a professional support system is a well-oiled communications mechanism, providing for inputs, outputs, and feedback responses. A NETWORK is closely parallel to the standardized communication loop familiar in business and journalistic lingo. The difference is that for the first time all the stick figures in the input, output, and feedback diagrams are women!

What Is a NETWORK?

CHAPTER TWO

While it is very tempting to attempt to define a NETWORK with a display of academic pyrotechnics delineating seven varieties of NETWORK theoretical structures, the truth is a lot simpler. A NETWORK is what its members say it is. Any group calling itself a NETWORK is a group involved in defining itself, rather than one obligated to fit into a predetermined structure. If a group names itself NETWORK, then so be it. The term is so common that it provides a broad umbrella for various sorts of organizations. The flexibility is all to the good, since there is no reason to construct a rigid model for a NETWORK and then require the varied and self-defining groups to fit the mold. I think a good deal of the fuss over NETWORK definitions, precise structure, and formalities is unnecessary, since groups should feel free to call themselves networks without any need to establish a right to do so. NETWORK is a useful term for diverse groups with certain aims. I would like networking to continue as a growing, expanding concept, even while I explore the motives, feelings, and emotions behind the decision of women to form a group that calls itself a NETWORK. I do not expect networks to stand still while being examined!

When people asked me why I chose the name for a group I helped to found in Bergen County, New Jersey, my first response was "Faye Dunaway." *Network* was one of the earliest recent, wide-appeal movies to show an ambitious, career-oriented, achieving woman executive. The implicit moral judgment, however, was negative: Faye Dunaway played a *nasty* woman who dared to discuss numbers, TV audience ratings, during sex. In this scene incidentally, *she* was on top, possibly the first Masters and Johnson influenced reverse missionary position scene in modern cinema. While I would not choose the Dunaway character as a desirable role model, this aggressive woman was new to recent cinema and, to those of us turned off by bosomy Stepford wives, a step in a positive direction. The movie and its heroine certainly influenced my choice of the term NETWORK, far more so than the legendary old boy NETWORK. I had in mind not a female imitation of male power structures, but instead a heroine of power, professionalism, and successful business behavior: a career woman to watch. Despite all the moral imperatives to view the Dunaway executive as unethical, power mad, and corrupt, I *liked* this woman's attitude toward her job. I did not find it any different from that of most of the successful men in business who have had to claw their way to the top, and I felt that she was the target of censure not because she exploited poor mad Peter Finch, but because *she* was the exploiter, or exploitress. I am not defending her unethical behavior; I am simply saying that dirty pool is dirty pool, and no grubbier when women wield the cue than when men do.

ROOM AT THE TOP

The sudden entrance of women into the business game room is the revolutionary impulse that lies behind networks. Why is it that suddenly, all over the United States, women are seeking to combine with other women in ways that have become so visible that they automatically draw censure? The NETWORK impulse is, in a very dirty word, a *power* impulse. It is an *elite* impulse. It is an *achiever's* impulse. And, to top it all off, it is a movement by women. The combined concepts of power, elitism, and achievement in business, are about as newsworthy as the announcement that millions of people went off to work this morning. Add the information that power achievement by an elite group is the result of *women* banding together in networks, and that's news.

The elitist nature of networks is new for women. The women in networks are those who are or want to be at or near the top in their careers; they are women of ambition, success orientation, and career motivation. The desire to form networks indicates a desire to tap into other women as resources, other women who can help them directly or indirectly by providing mutual support, career assistance, and useful business contacts. Women who get together in this way set out consciously to use other women and to gain their help, concepts which have been quite threatening up to now.

The reason these new groups are creating backlash is the tacit assumption that the NETWORK women are special: they are dedicated to their careers, they are job-oriented, they want to get ahead. They are women who are not afraid to label themselves *elite*, and are not afraid to apply words like *ambition, power, prestige,* and *status* to their desires. These words, used by women about themselves, represent a thrust which is new enough to attract attention and evoke fear in some men and women. For the first time in recent memory (I deliberately exclude the wonderful career women of the 1930s, since most of the women who form networks have had no exposure to Joan Crawford or Katharine Hepburn role models in real life), there are sufficient numbers of women achievers around to want to make contact with each other. The backlash is a tribute to the seriousness of the womanpower involved.

Women who have gotten to the top, and who have seen the process of career achievement as desirable and necessary, want to make contact with each other. That is the idea behind networks. Increasing numbers of women suddenly find themselves intrigued by the possibilities of rising to the upper echelons in business or the professions. They may not be in the executive suite yet; indeed they may be young women fresh out of school. But these women are perceiving success, and the power, prestige, status, and money that accompany career success, as positive goals. Their careers are a serious matter; the question of having to earn a living is secondary to the question of wanting to succeed. These women are not content to piggyback their dreams of success onto a current or potential husband's career; they want success and its benefits for themselves. As one highly respected and very well paid physician said, "If I wanted to be a handmaiden to a successful doctor, I'd be his nurse. What I want is to be a successful doctor." This is a very new motivation to action for women. The number of women who dare to announce business or professional success as a motivating force in their lives is small, but growing. This new, elite group of women is learning to NETWORK.

EACH IS UNIQUE

Because they are still few in number, these elite women must deal with the problem of isolation. Almost every woman who has made it up the career ladder has done so alone. Up until the last ten years, the successful woman was one of perhaps two or three in her profession or corporation. The current media hype, that women are making huge, quick strides to the top, is just that: a media hype. There are still relatively few women anywhere near the top as the top is generally measured: salary, title, status, and perks. By this yardstick, few women have yet achieved real success. Without trotting out every dreary statistic about women and work, I can safely say that if two percent of the executive force and ten percent of the professional work force are women, that is indeed a generous estimate. These elite women, then, are still very few both in terms of percentages of the whole, and in actual numbers. Because of the small numbers of women who appear in the professional or executive ranks, the feeling by each one that she is alone, isolated in her success, is an accurate one.

Every successful woman has her own story to tell. And it is probably a highly individualized story, with factors in it that are not yet quantifiable, despite preliminary studies indicating high success drives in elder daughters, for instance. But the uniqueness of the career-oriented woman does not have to doom her to isolation. Though her pattern may not be repeatable, or amenable to generalization, she need not stand alone or go through life unassisted. Again, that is what networks are about. The need by successful women to get together with other women of like achievement orientation and career motivation, lies behind networking. The women who have recognized themselves as unique have also simultaneously recognized that they need not exist in isolation from each other. Even unicorns can join together. While not abandoning their uniqueness, women achievers can combine to create the kind of support systems that they need as human beings. They can reach out to other women on the human level, but to other *elite* women. The successful woman needs alliances with other successful women. The desire to NETWORK represents a reaching out to achievement-oriented women by others of their kind, in order to share professional and personal concerns.

The move to NETWORK is not terribly democratic. The woman motivated to get to the top wants to find, and then associate with, other women like herself. She wants to NETWORK for mutual support with women who have gone through the same things personally and professionally. She wants to share experiences, brainstorm, and perhaps find coping solutions with other women with similar problems. Certain issues unite all professional women because they are women; these issues relate to balances between life and career that are unknown to men. Women in networks who have attempted to combine career, husband, children, and home invariably discuss the interchange between professional and life problems. One major problem that I have witnessed all over the country is, What does the professional woman do when the housekeeper fails to show up? Why is it that the children then become the mother's property and responsibility? One New York attorney was in Hong Kong on a business trip, and her doctor husband was at a medical convention in Chicago. Her son called her with the news that the housekeeper had to leave at once. The lawyer said, "Look, I am 8000 miles away; your father is 800 miles away. Call him, and tell *him* to come home!" This is a dilemma that is becoming more common. The woman who works for large sums of money as well as career achievement has very special problems to deal with if she also has a family. She wants to NETWORK to discuss these problems with other women in similar positions.

One topic of discussion that always appears when women in networks set up programs is, "The Balancing Act: How to Juggle the Demands of Career, Family, Home, and Husband." Women at a certain level of professionalism have genuine career demands made on them. And while no one has yet arrived at any final answers, there is great value in shared input on the questions. The point is that dual career families are so new that no clear patterns have yet emerged as role models. The sharing of responsibilities has to take place in the family, but no one knows exactly how this sharing translates into practice. Every woman in such a situation is a unique case, and each dual career household creates its own methodology. But the career woman can benefit from the experiences of other women facing the same problems. Networks enable these women to make contact with each other and provide mutual support systems with shared input.

BREAKING DOWN WALLS

The removal of barriers creating isolation in a period of social transition is a powerful enough impetus for networks of career women to form. We are now in a transitional time economically and historically, when career women, elite women, women achievers are too new to be categorized. But they each have to make it through their own lives, day by day, and they need a little help from their friends in the process. This kind of help can be found in networks. The women I am discussing, the ones I have met with all over the United States, want to know each other and use each other in career-determined ways; they need input from other women like themselves. The team spirit of, "I may be unique but I am not alone," is enormously helpful to the woman whom society still views as weird for daring to want success, whom other women may very well resent for having achieved success, and whom men may fear for announcing her determination to succeed. While it is said that no one likes a failure, I suspect the opposite in the case of women: no one really likes a success because no one knows what to do with her.

Because the successful woman is surrounded by traditional female envy as well as male hostility, it is doubly essential for her to find and associate with her peers. One woman in a regional NETWORK, an administrator in a graduate business school and the highest ranking woman on her campus, said, "The NETWORK meetings are my monthly therapy. I survive all the extraneous pressures in my life and career as best I can, but I look forward to being surrounded by other women who understand my problems and who can share war stories with me at these meetings." The experience of belonging and the availability of a time and place to share war stories, are powerful motives for the successful woman to want to join up with other successful women in networks. The elite woman needs these few hours a month with women like herself. She surely spends enough other time with other women, as well as with men and children.

COPING

So a NETWORK turns out to be a coping device: a mutual support system set up by women who help other women cope with a complex blend of career achievement and personal life. This is certainly a necessary and helpful sort of activity in today's complex and shifting world. There is, again, no reason why the career woman has to be a lonely tower of strength, an inventor of her own individual lifestyle, a standard-bearer for all women—and do it all by herself. It is normal, human, and acceptable for people of like interests to reach out to each other. The great strength of women is that they can do this so very easily. Women spontaneously form networks, share input, and help each other with an ease that has taken everyone by surprise. The surprise has been so great that criticism has been leveled at the instant friendship, the associations formed too quickly and too soon, and the insufficient development of long-standing ties in networks. I do not accept this criticism. It is the measure of the successful woman's strength that she can reach out to others, ask for sharing, and request help. It is the proud, aloof, solo high flyer who drops dead of a heart attack at forty-nine: *He* never asked anyone for help; he internalized his problems and literally died for want of a friend. Women do not have to repeat the mistakes of the achieving man. They do not have to, nor do they seem likely to want to, live in shells, outside of human warmth and comfort. Many women who have achieved great success want to maintain contacts with and draw input from other women for support. They recognize that they are unique, but they do not choose to function alone. They want to gain the assistance of other women, equally unique women, in networks, and to set up mutual support systems.

Unfortunately, the term *support system* is as bad an example of social science jargon as *sisterhood* and *consciousness raising* are of feminist verbiage. Yet all of these terms help explain what networks do. The formation of networks involves the sisterhood of successful women, whose consciousness is raised by establishing support systems with other like-minded women. Peer support in networks revolves around women providing sustenance to other women in similar circumstances. No matter what women are doing, they need to associate with other women in the same situation. This deep need for similarity in associations is the motive for women's networking on the same achievement level; the need for peer support is understandable and natural. Women need other women in similar life situations to share information effectively. Networks can provide the forums for women to trade help and support; they can provide the outer space, the time, place, and circumstances, for the sharing of inner space by these women.

WHEN THE ELITE MEET

Elitism is the most criticized aspect of networking. There is almost universal condemnation of those uppity women who dare to say that they are the new elite. Other women who are not success-oriented, as well as many men, have been highly critical of the elitist criteria in NETWORK formation. Women who have not qualified for membership have criticized the exclusionary principle. Men looking in from the outside have pointed to possible ripoffs, with women snookering other women through quick, shady deals made under the guise of friendship. Few outside the networks have recognized their value as elite peer support groups, which is the definition we are forming.

Why? What is wrong with an elite women's peer support group? Why is this bothering so many people? At first glance, the degree of negative reaction to networks seems disproportionate. The women in them are surely doing no harm to each other or to themselves. Networks have been formed by highly motivated women, who have spontaneously invented organizations for getting together. These various organizations, which show many similarities, obviously fill a need, since they have been created at pretty nearly the same time in various places, without interconnections among the creators. This phenomenal spontaneous generation is an indication that networks fill a new need. If many women in many places decide to join together to help each other in ways that are not even well defined at the start, obviously there are needs that cry out to be met in these women's lives. The very simultaneity of NETWORK development indicates that these needs are not being met by other groups, and so new alliances have to be formed on new bases. The major defenders of networks have been the women who form them. And the surprising vehemence of the attacks on groups which seem harmless enough requires examination.

There is apparently a lot of anger directed at women who have achieved success in careers, and at those who want to do so. Since the direct expression of this anger would be catty or unchivalrous, it finds covert expression in attacks on networks. Men and women alike are torn by ambivalence at the sight of a woman who dares to proclaim herself one of the elite. If too many women get too uppity, a revolution unparalleled in the history of the human race is going to occur. This is the source of the gut level fear: What happens if fifty percent of the human race decides that it wants the goals that previously the other fifty percent preempted for itself? If the female portion of the work force, hitherto content to stay out of the world of achievement except in small, token numbers, decides that it wants career achievement, the human race is in for a cataclysmic social adjustment. It is a natural human desire to avoid massive social upheaval for as long as possible. The spectre of large numbers of women forming networks and achieving career success haunts men and nonprofessional women. What is the world to do with such women when sufficient numbers emerge to force massive social change? Does the gathering together of these elite few, whose goal is to include more up and coming women in their ranks, portend a future too unknown, too frightening to be faced? Why not nip this trend in the bud, cut off the blooming networks, and so avoid a revolution?

It would be easier for women tied to traditional roles, and men tied to traditional role expectations, to avoid thinking of the revolution that is bound to occur when large numbers of elite women emerge; networks are not comforting entities. They inspire fear and distrust in men and women alike because they forecast disturbances in the status quo. At the very least, networks suggest that there are movers, shakers, and changers of the social order all gathering together. Networks gain much negative attention because they represent women who, if their views prevail, will be harbingers of countless and as yet unmeasurable changes. The millions of career-committed women not yet emerged will demand a reorganization of society far beyond anything yet seen in history. Networks represent the vanguard of women who insist on living in new ways; as the wave of the future, they are a threat to the status quo. People fear change and they are hostile to it; they are more comfortable with sameness. Thus, the formation of networks, merely as something new, inspires a great deal of anger in almost everyone *but* the women in networks.

THE HIGH FOR THE DAY

NETWORK members leave meetings feeling great. Almost everywhere, a NETWORK meeting is an up experience, even when strong disagreements occur or conflicts arise. Since networks are quite new and self-defined, a lot of the disagreements revolve around just what the group is supposed to be. The New Jersey NETWORK underwent a very difficult confrontation when one member insisted that we invite a housewife in order to keep in touch with Ms. Middle America. The idea had merit, but most of us did not feel that her suggestion was appropriate to the goals of our NETWORK. Despite the flared tempers resulting from the pro and con arguments, we still left that meeting feeling just as good as when we left meetings dealing with major substantive decisions, such as the one to publish a directory. The common denominator of a NETWORK meeting seems to be that all the members feel stronger, more confident, and self-assured afterwards. A kind of strength grows during these meetings that has nothing to do with the topics discussed; the strength is that of sharing ideas with women like yourself. What happens in NETWORK gatherings is a kind of sharing, a mutual input from women who take their lives and careers seriously, and this sharing gives each participant an added measure of confidence. This is also what networks are about.

Networks create a group high; being with women like themselves inspires new energy and confidence in the members. Simply the presence of ten or more women like you in the same room boosts your ego and sense of self-worth, and reaffirms your own value. There is a feeling of solidarity in the networks that brings out the best in each woman: her need to be fulfilled, as well as her gift to share. All women achievers have needs that have to be met; it is the male inability to express needs for nurturing, approval, and stroking that leads so many men to ulcers, heart attacks, and suicide. While women have traditionally been more able to express their needs, they have not been able to express needs for stroking on the professional level which networks can provide. Networks recognize a very new set of needs, a very new kind of support input that is desired. The women involved do not need reassurance about sexual or social desirability; this is no sorority or marriage mart. The women in networks are expressing needs in their *professional* lives; the support they seek is not on a personal, emotional, or psychological level, but on an external, professional level. The women in networks are saying, "Hey! We are all out there in the world. And we need some help in dealing with our everyday problems and choices in that world. We do not want crying towels or gripe sessions. We need to rub shoulders with other women on a professional, reality-oriented level." And this is found in networks. Of course there are discussions about clothing: in an era of galloping inflation, no woman who has any dealings with money could fail to notice that we seem to be approaching the prerevolutionary days in China, when a wheelbarrow full of yen was needed to buy a loaf of bread. But the small talk, chatter about clothing or food or children, is secondary to the sure knowledge that these women are talking to each other from a similar plateau. At any point, one or another of the women may say, "I had the most appalling morning with my assistant, Bill." This shop talk is exciting! The atmosphere of women talking shop is the most stimulating development that NETWORK observers notice.

There is a distinct high in the NETWORK room, the high of achievement. No matter what the topic under discussion, women recognize one another as peers, and feel the excitement of a new kinship group—the NETWORK. For perhaps the first time in history, women are meeting as representatives of a functional outside world. Women form networks based not on social or sexual exclusivity, reflected status, or inherited wealth, but on the kinship of earned merit and achievement. There is a community of goals, a team spirit, and the sure recognition that the other women in the room are also successful. No high compares to the recognition that you are surrounded by those like you, women with similar value structures, goals, and levels of achievement. Networks are acknowledgments that you are not the only successful woman on your block.

The spirit is that of a new clan, a new togetherness. A NETWORK is a community of interest, a group of women who share the success orientation and are proud of it.

INSTANT BUDDIES

One of the qualities in networks that involves their definition and is difficult for people to understand, is the suddenness of their formation. The logical question arises: "How can you throw a group of women into a room and expect them to bond instantaneously into a viable NETWORK of mutual contacts?" Instant bonding is a familiar enough phenomenon in our age. The real question is not, How can this kind of networking happen? but, What is its validity? How significant is the bonding of women who barely know each other, who do not have the long-standing old buddy kinds of ties that are present in old boy networks? Isn't there a kind of cavalier disregard for the time needed to build bonds of mutual trust, time that spans years, if not decades, of friendship? The argument is a pointed and serious one. Old boy networks take genera-tions to form—all those ancestors at Choate, Yale, and Harvard's "B"school. The problem is that women have not had this shared history. How could women's networks based on years of common associative ties develop? Until ten years ago women were not even present in the career world to any significant degree. Years of prep school ties are impossible. So networking on the old boy's time frame is impossible. This leaves women with two options. One is to wait a generation or two until there are sufficient women graduates from Ivy League schools and distin-guished business and professional schools to form a NETWORK in which jobs, favors, and promotions are handed out over breakfast or in the women's locker room.

Unfortunately we cannot wait for these things to happen; we need networks *now*.

The second option is to create, by means of instant bonding, new woman networks: artificial, formulated, consciously made association groups. The instantaneous forming of ties, bonds, and contacts is deliberate on the part of women achievers who recognize that they cannot wait, cannot deliberate over eons precisely because they do not have "world enough and time" to wait for networks to evolve slowly and naturally. Networks are being created, deliberately and quickly. Women are taking the risk of entering rooms where they barely know other women and attempting to form useful social contacts. It is highly conscious, artificial, and *necessary*. Can today's executive or professional woman, committed to her career, wait a generation until she knows her peers? No. The risk is too great. She risks losing the whole momentum in her own career and letting the present advantages she has won slip down the drain.

I am not defending the artificial bonding as the best of all possible measures. But given the choices of not networking at all, of waiting for women's networks to develop slowly and in the course of time, or of deliberately creating networks today, the last choice is best. Present acts solve present problems. The instant nature of networks, in fact, is really more of a paper dragon than critics have admitted. As another one of their strengths, women have always been able to socialize freely and openly on short notice. Perhaps because women have always been expected to create a social life for the family unit, they can now rather easily transfer their ability to socialize on a moment's notice into the NETWORK group. Of course there are variations of shyness and openness in any group of women in a NETWORK, but few problems have arisen along the lines of suspicion of instant buddies. Women are very ready to go out and meet other women. Confidence and trust take time to develop, but time can be measured in months or years, not generations. The speed of the NETWORK group formation has not created any problems except for male observers. Women are very willing to meet with other women in networks, on a professional career basis, and at least give them a chance. It may take time for deep trust and confidence to develop, but the idea of beginning the process by means of planned gatherings bothers no one except the outside critics, generally male, who feel that somehow this activity must be immoral.

Women realize that any help they gain from contact-making is a good thing. Even practice in the small art of exchanging business cards can be a very positive and necessary experience. To men, who have had long experience with business cards, the process may seem too simple to require practice. However, give the average male senior executive a directive to apply mascara, an equally simple task; then observe the results. It would be as difficult for a male senior vice president to apply mascara as it is for a female manager (without practice) to whip out a business card gracefully and give it to a recipient. Both procedures are acquired skills. The great work on the etiquette of business cards is still unwritten. And, to all of those men long accustomed to the many uses of a business card, I would point out that without generations of familiarity with the card, how is a woman to know these uses? The function of networks in educating and socializing women into the business world cannot be ignored.

Since one of the crucial problems holding women back in the business world is their very inability to socialize casually, on an old boy basis, their formation into networks as a practice ground for casual socializing must be helpful. Networks are, in many ways, training grounds for business socializing: the casual, friendly, "Wanna have a drink" associating that men are so good at. Women, who tend to zero in on deep, meaningful, intensely personal relationships, are learning how to take this skill, the ability to relate warmly to other women, and transfer it to the more casual, "hail-fellow-well-met" kind of socializing that networks call for. If there is one supremely important function that networks can perform, one main definition that fits, it is as a training ground for the nature and degree of contact-making necessary for business success. Networks teach women how to know, use, and get help from other women: how, in other words, to deal on a business, day-to-day level with other men and women. Women have to learn this deliberately and rather artificially because there has been no schoolroom in which to practice until now. The NETWORK meetings themselves are places where business manners can be perfected by those already in the game, a kind of finishing school for professionals. For women who have had to work hard to arrive at the top, who have not had precisely the advantages of years of learning old boy manners, the new woman networks are the places to learn. If networks do nothing more than that, they have succeeded.

Thus, networks enable the elite to meet, to support each other, and to learn and practice business palship. What is a NETWORK? It is what its members say it is. That definition best expresses the multiplicity and diversity of structures that are growing up all over, all calling themselves networks. As I use the term, as I see it used, a NETWORK is a gathering, on a regular basis, of an elite group of women who want to share and support each other in their professional lives. It may be the best thing that can happen to professional women who formerly lived in isolation, each thinking herself unique and alone, because it is a forum for the gathering of active, achievement-oriented women, not afraid of words like *power, ambition,* and *aggressiveness.* A NETWORK is a way these women can gather together, help each other, socialize, and learn to deal with their professional aspirations and the necessary sorting out of the many strands that go into a career woman's life. A NETWORK is a group of women who feel that each one is, in the shorthand of togetherness, *one of us*.

Beginning to NETWORK

CHAPTER THREE

Amalya L. Kearse is the first woman, the second black, and one of the youngest lawyers ever to become a judge in the United States Court of Appeals in Manhattan. And she does not eat lunch. The *New York Times* profile of Judge Kearse reads as follows:

> *In a recent interview . . . during lunch hour . . . she was sitting in her corner office at Wall Street and Broadway, for she rarely has time for lunch. "You work a lot, almost all the time, every weekend and evening," she said.*

This description of one woman achiever's lunch routine strikes at the heart of basic networking: the *lonely lunch syndrome*. This is to female executives what the locker-room syndrome is to males, and the initial impetus to NETWORK frequently begins with a simple lunch arrangement.

LONELY LUNCHES

Lunch is a key element in networking because at least ninety percent of women executives either skip lunch entirely, eat alone at their desks, or eat alone outside the office. A study of women executives at a major oil corporation headquarters in Houston showed eighty percent eating alone behind closed doors. Since only five women were of executive rank, it was easy enough to ask the one woman who claimed she did not eat alone what she did. She often ate lunch with her secretary. The professional loneliness implicit in not having a partner or destination at lunch hour is a powerful impetus for networking. If food is love, why should the female achiever be doomed to fast one-third of the time?

Lunch should be a break in the day, a time of sociability, a pause in routine that provides space for relaxation and refreshment of the mind as well as the body. How terrible for women careerists to pay the price of solitary confinement in their own offices simply because they have no one to eat with. Women in managerial or professional roles cannot easily break into male lunch groups: the men go out together, and it is awkward, if not impossible, to break into those groups. A woman may be tolerated once or twice, but as a regular lunch partner she will almost never make it into a men's group. A male corporate lawyer told me a story that illustrates the great divide. He set up a staff luncheon once every two weeks. The one female associate in his large legal department was of course invited; the lawyers discussed business, the corporation paid, the woman lawyer belonged. I asked him how the woman spent her lunch break on the other days, and he said, "Who knows? We all group together when we wash up, and I never see her at lunch time. She must be in the ladies' room."

For the lone woman lawyer to break into the male groupings would be a stress-laden activity on a daily basis; it is far easier to retreat to the ladies' room, law library, or one's own office. So women moving up the corporate ladder, or isolated in their own professional offices, use lunch time as an excuse to diet, existing on a container of yogurt in the closed-door office. What should be a pleasant break in the day's routine becomes a time to be avoided, a dreaded event. Skipping lunch altogether becomes a solution to a daily problem, and the lonely lunch syndrome goes on.

But the first woman who decides to break that syndrome can become the prime mover in a NETWORK. Every NETWORK I have seen has chosen lunch as the time to form contacts. Women are finally breaking out of their isolation and reaching out to each other for companionship, specifically at a meal time. Beginning to NETWORK is as uncomplicated as setting up a lunch date; that first meeting can be the prime force which eventually breaks down the lonely lunch and creates an atmosphere in which lunch can be an enjoyable part of the day, involving women who are like-minded and willing and able to share common concerns. Given the historic associations of women and food, and all the good relationships that occur when both food and fine conversation are shared, an ideal setting for networks is lunch time. My broker and I realized this on the first day we met to discuss business and ended up forming the embryonic New Jersey NETWORK. Our long first lunch ended with the mutual realization that we finally had achieved, if not in setting at least in style, the female version of the executive lunch.

THE EXECUTIVE LUNCH

Whether or not the NETWORK functions within a specific corporation or on an interdisciplinary level, the achievement of the executive lunch seems to be the first step in its formation. Both intracorporate groups, such as a nucleus of women in a large insurance company, and extracorporate groups, such as the interdisciplinary New Jersey NETWORK, cluster around the lunch meeting. Just as men find opportunities to socialize at lunch, women feel the need to do the same. The two-hour lunch is a standard way to set up the first exploratory meeting with interested women. While the two-hour lunch is not always possible, the commitment to it is extremely important: even if a woman is not yet on a career rung where she can take the time she needs at lunch, she can manage to make the time. Even if the nonexempt employee will be docked for lost time at work, if the group meeting is important enough to her, she will take that loss.

The one caveat, however, is in the group dealing with certain professionals: doctors and dentists quite often cannot spare two hours for lunch. In fact, medical people frequently have their own ideas about when lunch should be. One surgeon could not understand why our NETWORK was debating about lunch starting at 12 or 1; she begins her day in the operating room at 6 A.M., and her lunch hour is 11 A.M. at the very latest. Even within a corporation, the existence of flex time, international operations that run on different time clocks, and round-the-clock departments can make a shambles of what most people consider normal lunch time. Still the lunch meeting is the most appropriate and beneficial way to begin networking. The sheer feeling of executive power in being a part of a two-hour lunch is tonic to many women in management who have never really considered themselves managerial. And the presence of several other women able to take two hours for lunch also creates a feeling of power that is new and heady. While there is no reason to emulate the three-martini lunch and return to work potted, there is every reason to carve out a two-hour domain in one day, for openers, to begin the contacting process.

Who: That First Phone Call

The contacting process that begins networking is as simple as a phone call to set up a lunch date. Within a corporation, one woman manager may decide to call another to invite her to lunch; the immediate motive may not even be the formation of a NETWORK. It may be the human desire to talk shop instead of eating yogurt in secret. That first phone call can be a very hard step to take. There is always the fear of rejection, if not the actual possibility of it, which has kept women behind closed doors for a very long time. But once one person summons up her courage and decides to call another woman in management whom she knows, the results are almost guaranteed. The immediate occasion for shop talk will give rise to a sense of wonder, surprise, and delight at being able to share common concerns with another woman on a career level. One flourishing corporate NETWORK began when a manager called her counterpart in another department to find out how they could gain access to the men's shower room after jogging around the streets of lower Manhattan. To anyone who has run two miles under the defunct and drippy West Side Highway, the need for shower facilities is obvious. In this case, the presence of an underused but clearly delineated men's shower indicated a possible solution: the women managers were assigned certain days for using the shower facilities, the men, other days. And the by-product was a NETWORK group, nicknamed "The Dirty Dozen."

A NETWORK formed outside corporate walls or professional associations is more difficult to set up. The one phone call quickly escalates into more advanced logistics to determine who should be included. The *who* part of a corporate NETWORK is generally clear to everyone: the titles, number of employees supervised, and nature of responsibility is rather open knowledge, although there can be surprises when information is shared. Still, a corporate organization chart, job description manual, and operating procedure rules do make the selection of women on a similar level fairly straightforward. And the very few women managers are readily identifiable to each other. Unfortunately, there is still no real danger of embryonic corporate networks being overrun by women executives. Those women who want to group together know the others by sight. A rule of thumb is that you can expect no more than two percent of the executives to be women: even if a corporation has 1000 employees at one physical site, it is not difficult to pick out the twenty female managers. The first phone call can be followed up by interoffice memos, saving time and postage.

What: What Do Women Want?

When women in diverse fields begin to form an interdisciplinary NETWORK, the cry inevitably arises, "What do women want?" There is no simple answer to this. Interdisciplinary groups result from a variety of needs.

I was quite certain that an interdisciplinary group was necessary in Bergen County, New Jersey, because of geography: with certain exceptions, there are insufficient numbers of women in one particular career or industry to coalesce. There are a few very large corporations, and a few careers in which women are heavily represented —law, for instance—but for the most part, outside of major cities, women have to leave the borders of their own career or corporation simply to find enough other women to form a viable NETWORK. Within major cities there would certainly be sufficient women engineers, let us say, to form a Women's Engineering Association, or enough women in finance to form Financial Women, but even in this situation, there are advantages in networking out beyond the corporation or career.

The idea of an interdisciplinary group, cutting across the business, professional, and academic worlds, is attractive because of the diversity of input. The common bond is less one of particular professional concerns, although there is certainly a need for women to share those, than a clear level of achievement or aspiration within which women in various fields operate. In forming my own NETWORK, I felt that the ties of geography and of level of achievement were both essential. If we were to provide useful business contacts, we had to be within a realistic geographic boundary; if we were to have common grounds for discussion, we had to be at similar career levels. The kind of sharing possible if we expanded beyond our own professions or businesses was exciting: how many women college deans, for instance, knew women accountants? And how curious we all were about what the others were doing!

The model for our fledgling NETWORK was the Rotary Club; my stockbroker friend was nearly obsessive in her anger at being excluded from all the useful contacts Rotary provided. Short of storming the Rotary through a lawsuit, which would have been time-consuming, we were doomed either to be Rotariettes, or destined to build our own organization. We decided to build. Our decision was to select one outstanding woman from each field we could think of and to form a nucleus group by inviting these women to a luncheon. We felt that by proceeding in this way we would include as many career areas as possible, while ensuring a standard level of achievement. I remember feeling the lure of uncharted seas when we discussed women in careers as diverse as automobile body shop owners and nuclear physicists. This new adventure promised a vast opening-up of information about careers I had never thought of, and the possibility of meeting women doing unique and exciting work. When we finally met, the body shop owner expressed exactly the same idea: "I'm so glad I came to this lunch. I always wanted to hear exactly what college administrators *do* all day long!"

Why: Goals of the Network

Amazingly enough, the goals of virtually every NETWORK springing up either within a corporation or within one geographical area are the same: peer support, career information, and education. Of those three goals, peer support is the constant. The purpose of any group that sets out to meet under the NETWORK banner is shared support in concerns that affect women's working lives. Goal setting is the easiest part of forming a NETWORK: the women want to get together to support each other by sharing concerns during the work day, and sometimes after hours. We are all pioneers on a frontier where our very existence demands close-knit associations for mutual strength.

Although the media try to convince women that there are many role models and mentors out there, every one of us realizes that each woman is unique, an exception in her own right. Any woman who has risen to a position of achievement in business, the professions, or the academic world knows perfectly well that she had almost no rules to follow, no models to emulate, and few helpers. But although we recognize our uniqueness, we want to meet other career women for reassurance. An extremely important element of peer support is the need to know that we are not alone in career commitment, not freaks. We are all so used to being the exceptions, the tokens, that we feel out of touch with other women who have achieved success in other fields. Peer support is crucial to women just beginning to be felt as a force in the working world, and experiencing the problems of isolation, mistrust, suspicion, and envy. At our first NETWORK meeting, I was terrified of associating with women physicians and dentists. In my college days, women who went to medical school were considered strange, neurotic nonadjusters. I also experienced my own insecurities about a doctorate—would these "real" doctors snub me? The kind of support and strength that we all felt when we met was heartwarming. I was so impressed by the attractive, articulate, well-dressed dentist that I had to tell her to be sure to speak to young women, to convince them to enter dentistry. She, in turn, was surprised to find a sensible, practical college professor in touch with reality. The peer support was open and warm from the start.

Our first articulated goal was as follows: "Formation of an In-Group Support System, an old girl network, to receive input from successful women in the various professional and business communities—peer support for women on similar achievement levels, but in different work areas." And every other NETWORK I have seen has set forth very similar goals at the outset: the need to support each other, in whatever ways seem best at the time, is a constant. This support takes various forms, depending on the group: the women can share experiences ranging from sexual harrassment on the job to dressing for a television appearance. But whatever the topic, the goal of support—of providing a forum, an audience, a reservoir of goodwill—is always stated. It is the unique strength of women that they are able to ask for help; for almost the first time, women in careers have deliberately gotten together to ask for help from each other and have received this help generously in NETWORK groups.

The second goal, career advancement, is a spinoff from the old boy network. Every woman on a professional level knows that the best jobs are gained through contacts and connections, the *Who do you know* method. But every woman has not had access to this NETWORK for all the old reasons: exclusion from clubs, locker rooms, golf games. Women want to become part of the power structure, but can no more storm the barricades of the men's room than they can overturn Rotary rules. And so, the only practical alternative to entering the old boy network has been to form new woman networks. (I use *woman* because *girl* is demeaning for any female over fourteen.) The world of career commitments is still based on patriarchal modes; short of throwing cotton puffs at the hierarchy—ineffectual and time-consuming—women who want to enter the power game have to do so by combining, for there is strength in numbers. One goal of the NETWORK must be the free exchange of job information, so that women can use other women as contacts. This goal too is stated with remarkable consistency by almost all networks. In fact, at a recent meeting of a women lawyers' group, part of the roundtable introductions included informal job notices. Each woman present gave a short summary of the jobs she knew about. Interestingly enough, each summary began: "This job has not been posted yet," by the government lawyers, or "This isn't official, but there will be an opening in X department," by the corporate ones. The goal of informal contact-making to gain access to jobs that may never appear in print or in agency lists is easily achieved. Incidentally, the same process holds true for intracorporate networks: Ms. Manager of department *A* frequently can notify her NETWORK associates of job openings that never reach personnel.

The third goal, educational outreach, was formulated by the New Jersey NETWORK as follows: "Creation of an atmosphere in which women who aspire to success can meet role models. Formation of a speaker's bureau to sell achievement as a lifestyle. Meeting of NETWORK members to hear speakers in fields other than their own." Along with a desire to find and recognize other women like ourselves, we recognized the need to ensure a future. Most networking women are, in fact, set off from other groups of professional women by a sense of responsibility to the future; they do not want to be the last of their kind, an endangered species. The real possibility of career women losing ground exists. The latest statistics demonstrate a 0.8 percent drop in women in college administrative and professorial rank; a rise in women dentists during the past decade of 1.2 percent to 1.6 percent, which is equally negative; a drop in salaries of women as compared to men during the last ten years. Even to maintain a holding action, women have to ensure a new crop of women to follow their lead. One banker said that she personally felt obligated to supervise programs for upgrading her tellers, since without her direct interference, the typical bank pyramid—women in large numbers at the bottom, men in small numbers at the top—would remain unchanged. She commented, "I spend almost as much time identifying promising managerial talent among the women as I do deploying money. I know there'll always be a money supply in this bank. What I want to make sure is that another woman gets to run the show."

So the three goals of networks—the *why* of the groups that form—are peer support, career advancement, and educational outreach. In different industries, and different parts of the United States, one or another of the latter two may assume prominence. Among lawyers and financial women, well-developed job marts are being established; among educators, spreading the message to the next generation is stressed. In isolated areas, or smaller cities, both career and education goals merge: There are few achieving women already up there, and there is a strong sense of individual responsibility to the future. As I found from my counterparts in the midwest, the women who eventually networked were familiar with each other's successes and knew each other's names even before the first meeting. The realtor who was the organizer of one midwestern NETWORK said, "How could we *not* know who the other 'important' women were? The same twenty names are in every news story, and on the *Society* and *Style* pages as well. I've had to develop a set of casserole recipes to give to reporters: every time my corporation swings a huge land deal, someone asks me what I cooked that night." You can be sure that this corporation president is determined to educate the future generation of women business leaders.

But overriding all concerns with career information and education is the clearly stated goal of peer support. Those of us who decide to NETWORK, as opposed to joining existing groups or socializing on an unstructured basis, consciously make the decision to know and use other women as emotional resources. We reach out to share experiences and to create common bonds on a professional level, and to find out what others are doing and how they are handling decisions we all have to face. Whether the women are centered in one business, or represent a cross-section of as many areas as there are women to be found, the unifying thread is the need for other women with whom to discuss career-related problems and share career-related successes. The peer support is not a gripe session; it is an effort to create a basis for doing business together that includes sharing good news as well as bad. When an extremely able, but reticent, insurance company manager got her promotion to assistant vice president, the first people she called were her networking colleagues. They were delighted to hear of the promotion: they took her to lunch, bought her a small and very touching personal gift, and dropped by her office daily for the first weeks she was in her new job, just to provide her with moral support. The NETWORK closed ranks, became a team, and acted in unison behind the woman who had emerged as a leader. Their support made it possible for her to assume her new position with confidence.

When: Working It Out

After the NETWORK has agreed on *what*, *why*, and *who*, the practical decisions of *when* and *where* to meet must be tackled. The executive lunch club dedicated to peer support and career and education outreach has to come to grips with the mundane in order to move from the decision to NETWORK to the reality.

When is easier to tackle. Lunch takes place, generally, between 12 and 2, or between 1 and 3. I have found that the later hours work better: for some reason, the noon lunch is associated with clockpunchers. Perhaps one trait of executives is the ability to go for long periods of time without food, indicating a kind of moral fiber and/or dedication to work that surpasses the joys of eating. I am not at all sure why this connection takes place, but one very highly placed gubernatorial appointee, a department head in California's state government, was convinced that her M.B.A. was made possible by her ability to go for long periods without food. She worked her way through Stamford, and had no time between work and her classes; instead of eating in class or leaving work early, she simply skipped dinner for the years she was in school. If endurance is the key to the executive suite, then the later lunch is the classier one.

Of course, the *when* may be out of the hands of the networkers governed by staggered hours within one corporation. In a mammoth New York petrochemical company, there is simply no time other than 12 noon to NETWORK; there cannot even be a two-hour lunch, since the day is predicated on a three-quarter hour lunch break, and the concomitant work day shortened. In that case, the one and one-half hour lunch, starting a bit early, is what the original networkers had to work with. The point is, when women decide to get together within a corporate structure, they may be guided by sets of rules that are relatively inflexible; they must work within the firm's time scheme. In networking on a wider level, the *when* may also be predetermined by the wider social context of the professions involved and the local geography. The surgeon who started work at 6 A.M. could not survive beyond 11:30 without lunch. Psychiatrists must often wait until at least 2 P.M. to eat, since they can see at least two patients during their patients' lunch hours. If the executive lunch is to include professionals and academics, the *when* has to be flexible. Sometimes lunch must be scheduled at a time when certain women in the group can never be there. The only ways to finesse that are to hold occasional dinner meetings, to keep in touch on a less formal basis than lunch meetings, and to send minutes and notices to the absent members. No matter what time you set up, someone who should be there just won't be able to.

A second facet of *when*, and one which is far easier to deal with, is how often the networks should meet at first. By common consent, the meetings are almost invariably on a monthly basis. The particular day is less important than the decision to set up a *regular* day: every second Wednesday, for instance. Some experimenting will be necessary to determine which day is best, but once the day is decided upon, the setting up of a regular schedule is important so that NETWORK members can allocate their time on a predictable basis. Knowing there will be a long lunch meeting on the second Wednesday of each month enables the member to plan other career and personal activities in advance. In certain geographical areas, care must be taken to avoid conflicts with other groups, such as Women's Forum meetings in Denver. Scheduling conflicts with established professional groups, such as the Women's Division of the American Medical Association, should be carefully avoided. With members' willingness to juggle commitments, a reasonable amount of experimenting, and a lot of goodwill, the *when* can be settled.

Where: Out to Lunch

I have saved the *where* for last, since it has been the most difficult issue to settle for beginning networks. This problem, where to meet, returns us to our original story of Judge Kearse and her decision not to eat lunch. Where can a group of serious, business-minded women go to eat lunch in an atmosphere conducive to a relaxing, pleasant, productive meal? The only immediate answer is a men's club, but that is the problem, not the solution. The solution, as we will see, has been the founding of NETWORK lunch clubs, but for the opening meetings, that is not a practical goal. Every starting NETWORK, whether inside a corporation or in a limited geographical area, has begun lunching in incredibly poor surroundings. The first meeting of the nucleus of the New Jersey NETWORK took place in a local restaurant known for good hamburgers; the hamburgers were delicious, but the spot was dark, rock music interfered with conversation, and the large bar was populated by married "singles" trying to score over the lunch martini. The closely packed tables provided us with some vocal and not very welcome additions to our group. There we were, briefcases on our laps, trying to write up some goals and lists of members, and blocking interference from men at the next table who could not fathom a business lunch conducted by four women. I decided they were right: no one could conduct business in a dark, smoky, noisy room in a public place. At times like those, I longed for the Harvard Club.

As an interim step, we took over the conference room in the law offices of the women lawyers who were part of the founding mothers' group; we had no other options, and we were fortunate to have such a setup available. The disadvantages were the messiness, the lack of waitress service, and the general disturbance caused by passing food around while trying to talk and listen. But the advantages were privacy, more comfort than a public place, and a lack of pressure to order, pay, and eat up.

A group within a corporation can make a bid for the partner's conference room, or any suitable, available room. Food can be ordered, or members may bring their own. Most important is that the atmosphere be conducive to business: talking, listening, writing. Activities connected with food should be unobtrusive; this is not the time to experiment with fondue. If a conference room is not available, a specific table or area in a company cafeteria might be reserved for the group. Though not private, it is a clearly delineated place, with enough room for papers, and as little hassle about food-passing as possible. The optimal solution is a private room; short of that, a table in a communal dining room will do. Never hold meetings in a member's office: that will do untold harm, by raising everyone's suspicion level. A secret lunch meeting, which is what it will look like, can destroy both corporate goodwill and managerial credibility. It is better to go to the local hangout than to meet in any fashion that smacks of secrecy.

For groups that form outside one corporation, the *where* is more difficult; there is not necessarily a law partnership with a conference room available. In fact, at one formative meeting of a Women's Bar Association group that wanted to NETWORK out to other groups, all the difficulties of place emerged. We met in Manhattan's Chinatown, on the top floor of a restaurant. Unfortunately, the top floor was not private; we had three tables of eight women in one corner, and about the same number of diners in the rest of the room. Obviously, cross talk between our three tables was very difficult; and the speaker—me!—had to address a room divided between women lawyers interested in networking, and some poor souls who merely wanted to eat lunch. In addition to the physical difficulties inherent in an uncomfortable situation the ordering, passing around, and paying for the food was both difficult and time-consuming. It is extremely hard to NETWORK between moving platters and whispering speakers. A temporary solution might be a private club that needs some extra business at lunch hour. The place must be conducive to relaxation, sharing ideas, and conducting business: food, service, atmosphere all have to lead to those goals. At the start, I can only suggest a private room in corporate headquarters, or a private room in a club or restaurant, since any public place is simply too distracting for business.

SUMMARY

Networks in formation have to consider the five *w*'s: *what*, *who*, *why*, *when*, and *where*. There is a remarkable consensus on *what*: networkers almost always form a lunch club. *Who* is also relatively simple: the visible executive women within a corporation, or professional, academic, and business women who contact each other on a geographical basis. Like it or not, the women who found networks seem to recognize each other by something almost akin to telepathy: they home in on each other as if equipped by radar. That first telephone call inevitably leads to the first meeting. *Why* is clearly peer support, an almost unanimous goal; next come career mobility and educational outreach, generally in that order. *When* settles into a one day a month, two-hour lunch time slot. *Where* is more difficult, since it must be at the very least private, quiet, and convenient.

In the beginning, the sense of accomplishment in having set up an embryonic network with relative ease, cooperation, and good vibes gives the women involved a tremendous sense of unity. After our first lunch meeting, despite all of the drawbacks in the place, the nucleus of four women experienced a sense of euphoria summed up by the stockbroker: "After four years of working here, at last I have someone to have lunch with and talk business to who is not involved in sex and power games. It's a great feeling to talk real talk to interested women." Networking involves real talk, real business, real women, real work: it is the beginning of the future.

Organizing
the First Meeting

CHAPTER FOUR

Creating the first NETWORK lunch meeting is a little like giving birth for the first time: you know you have to push hard to bring the baby out into the world, but you don't know what the both of you are expected to do afterwards. (Perhaps the analogy to birthing is the reason the charter members of the New Jersey group became the *founding mothers*.) After giving birth to this exciting new entity, we turned to each other and said, "Now what?" The answer, the first step in networking out, is contacting women outside the founding nucleus. After the basic *who, what, when, where* and *why*, have been settled, a first meeting of a larger group has to be planned. In our case, only four women were involved in setting up the NETWORK; in other situations, as few as two have been prime movers, especially within a single corporation. In order to organize the first meeting, however, a larger group has to be gathered: at least eight women, and at most twenty-five, represent workable limits for the fledgling group.

THE NUMBERS GAME

Fewer than eight women forms a very weak base for any kind of help or power structure; the input is too limited. Had we four kept to ourselves, we would have dispersed in a short time: the stockbroker was insistent on imitating Rotary, I was overly academic and theoretical, and the lawyers were running out of patience with us both. But although four women do not a group make, more than twenty-five leads to the opposite danger: overloading everyone's circuits with too much input and diversity. Crowding can lead to fragmentation, splits into smaller cliques, and charged tempers. The basic management efficiency rule of no more than ten people on a committee should be stretched, but not too far, and adopted by networks. Between eight and twenty-five women is an ideal starting group.

The number of women involved is often determined, not by the ground rules of basic management, but by reality. If there are only six women executives in a corporation, then only six can be involved in the NETWORK of women managers at that site. In fact, at a very large investment banking house, only five women could be found in any position above the rank of executive secretary. Since only two percent of the executive suite is occupied by women, the smallness of numbers is not surprising. In certain geographical areas, there are still very limited numbers of women achievers in any work area at all. While this may be changing, certain realities often dictate the numbers of women eligible and available for networking. An ideal number does not exist. Networks deal with the real number of women in any given realm.

RISK, REWARD, AND REJECTION

All founders have to conquer the fear of giving a party to which no one comes, and the other possibility of having too many people show up. Organizing that first meeting sets in motion certain fears, risks to be taken, and decisions to be made. Depending on the kind of networking being done—within a corporation, a professional group, or a geographical area—the kinds of outreach to potential members varies. There are always risks, especially at the beginning when the women are unknown to each other. If these risks are seen clearly in advance, the whole process becomes easier. At the end of every risk, we are taught in business school, lies a possible profit or loss: the risk has to be weighed on that basis. The question is, "Will the risk pay off on the bottom line?" But since operating on a management risk and reward basis is new to women, the purely business risk factor takes on a personal element. Risk to women is tied, not to the bottom line, but to fears of rejection.

One of the risks in starting a NETWORK is the rejection of the entire concept by any of the women approached. One young sales manager in a computer software house turned a cold shoulder to an older woman manager trying to set up a NETWORK by saying, "I'd never waste my time with a bunch of women." There are queen bees everywhere, and at every age. But a single negative response should not be taken as a signal for the networker to fold up her tent and go home; it is merely an indication that one woman is not interested. Perhaps the nay-sayer opposes all groups; in this democratic society, one of the options we have is to be a nonjoiner. There are, in fact, large numbers of women who refuse even to vote. The embryonic group cannot wilt or undergo agonies of self-doubt because one person, even two, are not in favor of it.

A very aggressive, articulate real estate operator, with an M.B.A. degree, who developed syndicates for building ownership and management, came to one of our first meetings. She did not participate and left her blank questionnaire at her seat. When I called to ask her opinion about the group, she informed me that the group was time-wasting, goalless, unstructured, and unhelpful; we did not even have plans for acquiring our own building to create a clubhouse! I took her criticisms seriously and began to have doubts about the entire NETWORK project, because she was an expert in management and a shrewd businesswoman. I was feeling rather dubious until, at the next meeting, my fellow networkers turned on me to demand why I had brought such a cold, authoritarian, female male chauvinist into our group. They all felt that she lacked the kind of warmth and social responsiveness that makes the casual social interplay of networking possible. So, risks can bring rewards and rejections. One nay-sayer has to be taken in stride, and can even consolidate the more positive group members.

STICKING TO YOUR OWN KIND

Within a corporation, the process of beginning to NETWORK is fairly simple, at least from a communications viewpoint. Since the women involved will all be on the same premises, the obvious means of communication is the interoffice memo. The founder can simply write down the date, time, place and purpose of a meeting of executive women, and send off a memo. The real question is, "To whom do you send the memo?" The basic rule for beginning to NETWORK within a corporation is "stick to your own kind." Managerial women must stick with other managerial women; supervisors with supervisors; secretaries with secretaries. What counts is the level of employment: *rank*. A NETWORK is not egalitarian, for reasons that have internal as well as external validity. Peer support can exist only among peers; and, as discussed further on, no NETWORK group should run the unnecessary risk of triggering management fears.

Women on the managerial level who want to get together with other women managers can identify them quite clearly because there are so few. Even in huge corporate headquarters with thousands of employees, the small group of managerial women is easily spotted. If by some remote chance there are more than twenty-five women managers, a logical division can be made between line and staff women. This point is highly theoretical, since I have not yet run across a corporate NETWORK threatened by inundation of executive women, even in industries where women abound, such as cosmetics and retailing. When head counts are taken, the same two percent (a generous figure, by the way) of executives turns out to be female. So if there were one thousand middle managers, there would probably be twenty women who could NETWORK within the corporation. This is still far more than can really be found in almost any industry. One corporate manager, who prides himself on his interest and helpfulness in women's careers, was complaining that because of changes on the executive level, the tone of the management meetings had changed drastically for the worse. He said, "And can you imagine? Everyone comes to meetings in shirtsleeves these days. Whatever happened to the vested suit?" I asked, "What do the women wear?" He looked totally blank, and then cheered up slightly: "We don't use a secretary any more. The proceedings are taped." So women managers need not fear a NETWORK weighed down by numbers.

The motive for sticking very strictly to one level of achievement and seeking peer support among peers is to avoid triggering top management suspicions. If managerial women start to create movements within a corporation involving technical and clerical personnel, the word that will occur to male managers is *union*. In fact, in a NETWORK I observed at a major surburban company headquarters, this is exactly what happened. The networking movement was not only completely unrestricted as to the level of women involved, but also not even limited to women: men were invited as well. About five hundred employees, mostly women, were counted as members, and the prime motive of the NETWORK was peer support, career advancement, and sharing of input on both job-related and personal problems. The five hundred broke down into much smaller groups, tackling problems as diverse as "The Dual Career Family," and "Coping with Divorce." Meetings took place at lunch hour, on company premises; the organizers were highly placed women executives who wanted to involve all of the women in mutual self-help efforts without excluding the men.

These motives were quite laudable; in the best of all possible worlds, management would be delighted at the spectacle of large numbers of employees turning out, on their own time, to help each other. But in this situation management immediately suspected sub rosa unionization efforts; the organizers were given little cooperation, and their budget mysteriously shrank. In fact, the original networkers finally had to do all the work of setting up meetings, sending out notices, placing posters on the bulletin boards, and keeping track of group activities on their own time, because management had became so suspicious. Instead of the founding women's gaining a reputation for managerial ability and dedication to the company by founding a NETWORK beneficial to the corporation, quite the opposite happened. The entire NETWORK was viewed as subversive, and the rank and file was infiltrated by top-level male management, not for networking purposes, but for surveillance. The leaders were forced to omit their NETWORK activities from their resumes in any career advancement they sought within the corporation. Remnants of the NETWORK exist today, but the atmosphere is so negative and charged with hostility that its usefulness is questionable.

PARANOIA AS A LIFESTYLE

Why this paranoid corporate reaction to a roomful of women meeting to help each other? Because, realistically, no management group can be expected to react to a meeting of several hundred women with anything but deep fear and suspicion. In addition to their overt fears of a few managerial women leading an army of file clerks into unions, there is the deep-seated fear men have of women. This fear is a constant in western civilization: if any one emotion has governed male-female relationships, it has been male fear. While it is beyond the scope of this book to explain that fear, women who want to NETWORK have to understand that male management cries of "unionization" represent deeper fears men have about women. And, although nonunionized office women are an exploited group, the idea is to gain management's cooperation in networking, not to set off hostile and destructive feelings. Until it can be proven that there is some point in antagonizing the male power structure, corporate networking should be done with tact, goodwill, and caution.

Networking is a process that goes on in the real work world. In this real world, men dominate, yet fear, their women employees. The men are not ogres or evil-intentioned male chauvinists. By and large, the male executives are fiftyish or older and bewildered by the sudden emergence of women into a previously all-male arena. The male executives do not understand what is happening: Why didn't this turn out to be the world their fathers led them to expect? If any women's NETWORK is to succeed, it cannot give the appearance of being an effort to unionize, since that will only trigger the male boss's suspicions of his secretary's loyalty. He will welcome the NETWORK about as enthusiastically as he would welcome the idea of paying his spouse for homemaker's services. The only way to gain male management's cooperation, and avoid hostility, is to keep the networking women strictly on the same executive level. If executive women choose to lunch with each other one day a month and make the effort to sell this idea to management as a benefit to both the women and the corporation, senior management's fears of unionizing can be allayed. Is this a kind of Aunt Tomism? I think not. The issues of networking and unionization are quite distinct. Networking deals with women on the same level using each other's expertise, moral support, and skills for personal and career purposes. Unionization has always meant organizing for economic gains. While unions wish to change the structure to benefit the workers, networks function within an existing structure to make the most of it. Unions are revolutionary, and networks evolutionary, and never the twain should meet.

One key aspect of networking should be its openness: emerging unions function in secret, but networks should begin in the most open fashion possible. The start of a NETWORK ought to be like giving birth on television. Within a corporation, the interoffice memo sent to women managers by the NETWORK founder will, of course, be seen by everyone. There is no such thing as an office secret of this kind; even the copying machine has eyes. And secrecy is undesirable. The idea is to reassure top management that something positive is going on, not to arouse suspicion. It cannot be stressed too often that men fear womanpower: women who have power, and then combine with other women, terrify every male in sight merely by their presence. One networker in a media corporation learned this through painful experience. Euphoric after her first NETWORK meeting, she returned to her office, and was immediately met by her boss, who had been awaiting her return. He asked, "Well, which of us guys did you ladies roast today?" The woman manager was shocked by the level of mistrust, anger, and suspicion that the man showed. Fortunately, she realized that most men suspect any women who meet together of attacking "the guys," and she was able to resist answering. But after closing her office door, she cried in frustration at the warped communications between men and women. Are the male fears paranoid? Yes. Can they be ignored? No.

RESERVING THE BOARD ROOM

Since the interoffice memo inviting women managers to the first meeting will be common knowledge within the hour, one way of acting openly is for the networker to discuss the first meeting with the most senior-level male manager involved. A perfect way to initiate this discussion is to request the use of the corporate board room for the first meeting. While this suggestion has met with gasps, the logic is quite simple. The nucleus NETWORK should aim for corporate cooperation. This is a simple goal, but to get it, the game has to be played by the power rules currently in operation. If it will do more harm than good to meet secretly, send out confidential memos, and create suspicions of subversive activities, then there is absolutely no point in so doing. For a woman manager to have to ask permission to lunch with colleagues may be demeaning, theoretically. But if we forget about theory and deal with the real corporate world, asking can be a tool for the good. The onus of requesting a blessing on one's lunch partners can be removed by asking for something tangible: use of the board room or conference room.

A perfect way to unite legitimacy of purpose, solve the ever-present problem of where to hold the lunch, and invite the women you want to invite by interoffice memos is to request the corporate board room for the first meeting. This request involves an extraordinary act of courage on the part of the woman manager who decides to do it. It will be her task to explain why she wants this normally male preserve, who will be using it, and what the purpose will be. Even if the request is refused, making it alerts male management to what the women are doing. It is a wedge that can be used to explain networking to male colleagues and superiors. If management cooperation is won from the outset, the corporate NETWORK can begin in the right way; management cooperation will never be won if networking is not explained. And the beauty of requesting the board room is that it may very well be granted! Management cooperation can easily turn to permission to use the room regularly, funding for the lunches, and payment for speakers. If top management is won over, the NETWORK within a corporation will turn out to be a tremendous force for good. At worst the present request to use the board room will be denied, and if the networker is persistent, she will press for a future date when the board room will be available. In the current climate of doing something for women—and men are truly bewildered by what they should be doing—such a request is often granted.

Thus, circulation of the first interoffice memo to same-level managers, and announcement of NETWORK intentions to senior management via a request for use of the board facilities for lunch, is the best way to get the corporate NETWORK started. It is efficient, quick, and workable:

all of the women are reachable in the same place with a minimum of effort. And the way is paved for corporate co-operation, and perhaps financial assistance as well, by the nucleus networkers' ability to show benefits that will be gained if the women managers are unified. Corporate anxiety about unionization, as opposed to executive-level unity, can be diffused by sticking to the elitist concept —women at a certain management level—from the start. In many ways, the corporate NETWORK is the easiest one to bring to birth. And if the board room is gained as a regular meeting site, the whole subject of lunch can be solved, in ideal fashion, at least on that once monthly basis. One corporate NETWORK on Wall Street, an area known for lack of eating places as well as lack of tolerance for women, now has full use of a magnificent corporate conference room for one luncheon a month, catered by an outside food service concern and paid for by the corporation. How did this happen? It happened because two networkers summoned their courage and asked for use of this room for a managerial women's group. As the instigating founding mother remarked, "When the president said, 'You mean that's *all* you want to do, have lunch brought in to the conference room so you can meet together? I thought at least you were asking for a second conference room to be built!' I realized how foolish we women were in being afraid to ask for things." The NETWORK can begin in an atmosphere of hospitality and warmth if the founders show confidence, openness, and honesty in their methods and goals.

PROFESSIONAL GROUPS

Beginning a NETWORK of professional women who are already organized in their own profession or industry but are eager to reach out to other organized women's groups, does not involve any male fears of unionizing, but it does involve different kinds of birth pangs. Women's reaching out to other women, no matter how the move for peer support is organized, is a painfully self-conscious act. When a few members decide to NETWORK within an existing organization, such as the Women's Bar Association, the Business and Professional Women's Association, or the Women's Coalition for Higher Education, the spreading of the word is quite straightforward. The organizer simply places an announcement of a meeting—time, place, date, purpose, and R.S.V.P.—in the journal or newsletter that already circulates. The advantage of an existing organization is that a line of communication is ready-made: the New York Women's Bar Association, for instance, has a bulletin. When a decision was made to form a NETWORK group, a luncheon announcement was placed in the bulletin. To aid planning, a telephone number for reservations was included in the announcement. A room in a restaurant was reserved on the basis of the replies, and about twenty-five women showed up at the first luncheon. Obviously, the number had to be ascertained in advance to enable the luncheon planning in terms of the size of the room reserved, the seating arrangement, and the costs. A futher refinement suggested by one of the original members was a set menu: something simple and appealing to everyone, such as a chef's salad in summer or chicken dish in winter, facilitates conversation by removing the need to look at menus, deliver orders, and instruct waiters. At one such luncheon I attended where there was no set menu (and the food was Chinese), most of our time was spent ordering the dishes, figuring out who got what, passing around the rest for everyone to try, and finally paying a bill the length and complexity of General Motor's annual budget. There was little room for any serious conversation. At the next meeting a chef's salad was ordered, eaten, and enjoyed by all; the bill was split; and maximum networking took place with a minimum of fuss.

The first step for professional women in organizations is a simple one: one person takes charge of not only the luncheon planning, but also the announcement, the site selection, and the reservations. Because there are not that many women involved, no real delegation of responsibility is needed at this point. There will be the usual problems in planning for groups: Will the right number of women show up? What about the ones who make reservations and don't show? What about the ones who don't make reservations and *do* show? Professional women are no different from other people, and there will be the usual number of no-shows and no-reservations. At one women's medical group meeting, two members had to share what was, fortunately, a huge spinach, bacon, and mushroom salad because one more woman attended than had responded, and a set number of lunches had been ordered. Since the atmosphere was so good, no one really minded, and to settle accounts, the woman who came in last paid the tip. With twenty women, the food and arithmetic were simple.

Dinosaurs Dancing

The problems that an extant organization has to deal with are not difficulties in reaching its own membership: that mechanism is already set up. The real problem is outreach to other professional organizations. And that involves a degree of decision-making and self-exploration that cannot be rushed. Generally, professional women within an organization tend to be crisply goal-oriented: associations of women deans, lawyers, and advertising executives are quite used to decisiveness and activism. I would caution such groups not to move *too* quickly: over-eagerness to reach out before the group has cohered can cause disintegration of the entire process. Networking is a subtle group-formation activity, and there is a great deal to be said for unpressured group interactions among people who are already known to each other, even if only by being in the same profession, before any kind of reaching out to other, equally organized, professional groups takes place. Any problems within the networking group must be aired and talked out before outreach to another group begins: if this is not done, internal divisiveness can foul up the whole project. The first task for the professional women is to get to know each other: a group of academic women turned out, at the very first NETWORK meeting, to be so sharply divided between administrators and faculty members that an outreach program to the local Business and Professional Women's Club had to be postponed for almost a year. As one counseling director said, "We are such academic fuzzies that neither the teachers nor the deans seem able to cope with budget problems as opposed to personality conflicts. How on earth can we join forces with women in business when our own houses are in such disarray?"

The most fundamental step for a group of women in the same profession who decide to NETWORK is getting to know each other, and comparing goals and purposes before contacts are made with other groups. Since networking is in so many ways a feeling-out of other women's professional expertise as well as a bid for emotional and career support, there is more than enough to discuss at the first group meetings of women within professions who specifically want to NETWORK. If women bankers, for example, as a NETWORK nucleus feel that any nonbusiness contacts would waste a lunch hour, it would be folly to throw this group in with fledgling editors who may not only be ineligible for any loans at present, but also be unable to afford so much as a healthy savings account.

The nature of the interested NETWORK members must be gauged with accuracy and sensitivity—each woman has to take the measure of her tablemates—before the leaders contact other groups. The risk in too speedy an outreach program is a hasty, and inevitably short-lived, marriage of opposites who have little in common.

If we think of groups as if they were dinosaurs, and in many ways all structures have a kind of pterodactyl unyieldingness and rigidity that simply comes from the organizing effort and discipline needed to attract and retain members, we should realize that one dinosaur loping along the plains is improbable enough. Calling in a second one to start the waltz may just be the kind of effort that tramples everything in sight! No one really knows yet whether organizations as disparate as financial women and medical women can provide peer support and mutual sustenance to each other. The whole process of networking is far too new to be able to provide statistics detailing the outcome of throwing organized groups of women at each other. The most sensible first step—since dinosaurs *may* dance quite gracefully—is for the group to examine itself: its members, its goals, and its aspirations. An arbitrary, but not unreasonable time limit for intragroup explorations is six months; in that amount of time, the women in a professional group who want to NETWORK can share each other's space before they make outside contacts. Then they can ask for the next waltz.

Thus the networking group within a professional group is the easiest one to organize: a bulletin already exists for dissemination of meeting notices; the membership list is available; and structures have been formed for announcing meetings, accepting reservations, and keeping track of interested members. To NETWORK with professional women outside their own fields, organization members should be well-organized, and they should have some prior contacts with the other women. The worst kind of networking fiasco I have ever seen took place when a group of publicity women chose to contact a group of insurance women. The insurance women were mostly in sales; the publicity women were mostly in public relations. The lunch table buzzed with selling: every woman seemed to be pushing her product, herself, and her company. There was virtually no sense of common goals or mutual support because there was no atmosphere of trust, low-key input, or prior ties. Fifty superstars in a row emitted too much dynamism for any group to cohere, and the nucleus NETWORK dissolved in a blur of animosity. The last muttered comment was, "Who ever said that *men* were the only con artists?" Speed kills, in more ways than one.

GEOGRAPHICAL NETWORKS

Bringing a Buddy

The last kind of NETWORK, the geographical one that crosses professional, academic, and business lines, is probably the most difficult one to organize at first: it is closest in spirit to a men's club, and as such operates with rules that are neither clearly understood nor easily accepted by women. The first difficulty of the geographical NETWORK is that there is no established means of communication. No company headquarters provide a common workplace, and no bulletin provides a ready-made communication vehicle. The point, in fact, is the very diversity that each member brings to the group; efforts are made to include women from all fields of business, any and all professions, the academic world, even arts and politics. When diversity is the goal, the organizing process is both diffuse and difficult. The principle can only be set forth as "bring a friend."

When my three cohorts and I decided to found a New Jersey NETWORK, we tried to structure the "bring a buddy" approach in order to enhance the diversity and to prevent an overloading of the group by any one kind of member. I was told, jokingly I think, that no other college administrators would be allowed, and under no circumstances another professor; I had to convince my three partners that there were other academic women who could function in the business world. Still, at a recent membership meeting, a professorial networker was vetoed because she was deemed too much a schoolmarm. She had attempted to take over the meeting, only her second one, and had tried to run it like her classroom. I shall deal with membership criteria later on, but our group began by listing prominent women we knew in any field we could think of: retail store ownership, realty sales, graphics design, medicine, government service, theatrical design, and others. The operating principle was the Rotary one—one member from each profession—but we had to stretch this considerably to allow both for outstanding women within the same profession, and entire areas where no professional women could be found. For instance, we listed a number of physicians, but all in different specialties: surgery, pediatric urology, dermatology, and others. But we never found any industrial production managers or even one engineer within shouting distance.

We attempted to list fields and women, to see how we could match up the names, and whether, in addition, we knew other qualified women. That sounds quite informal, but really was more structured. I had access to the federal job classification guide materials in my college library, so I worked out the kinds of job areas that were relevant: on the managerial and professional level, for either sex, that is an underwhelming task. The other women—two lawyers and a stockbroker—knew more women in the geographic area than I did, and they plug-ged names into the categories I had listed. We met for this session at lunch time in a restaurant owned by a woman, and did our bartering in a very tearoomy sort of atmos-phere. I would call out the title, "advertising director," they would counter with a name, and the waitress would ask whether we wanted more popovers. Through this game of "Who do you know," "What does she do," and "Would she be interested in a NETWORK," we arrived at a list of two dozen women we would like to see in the group.

Armed with this list, we then had to contact each woman personally to explain the NETWORK idea and to invite her to lunch. Without a bulletin, a common work-place, or an interoffice memo, this took a great deal of time and effort. We had decided upon the lawyers' conference room as the best lunch spot: at that juncture, no restaurant could be found that was both convenient and suitable. We really wanted a lunch place owned, or at least operated, by a woman. Not finding that, we settled on the confer-ence room and a brown bag luncheon.

After deciding on the place, the day, the date, and the time (the two-hour time slot was clearly delineated as 1 to 3 P.M.) we then had to notify each woman on the list. Each of us had a minimum of six phone calls to make, in which we not only had to set forth the particulars, but also the whole idea of networking, and then listen to various argu-ments, agreements, and problems about time, place, and circumstance. This is where the birth of an organization represents a long labor of love. Any more than six personal contacts per member is too demanding in terms of time and the increased risk of rejection. Any woman contacted may respond (as one did): "Don't be absurd. Why would I want to join a lunch bunch? I can eat with women in Bloom-ingdale's if I really want to." However, there are also rewards: the fourteen women who showed up at the first luncheon have remained valuable and enthusiastic members.

After the initial phone calls, there remained a necessary followup: we had to send out a mailing (thanks to the lawyers' secretarial staff), confirming the time, place, and date, and reminding the women to bring lunch. Verbal discussion must, as a general rule, be followed by written confirmations, plus a request for reservations. Never trust anyone's memory, I have found, when you are planning a lunch: at the very least, we had to make sure that enough chairs were placed around the conference table. Predictably, several women who originally said they could attend Wednesday at 1 P.M. were called away on business and did not attend. Of the two dozen women invited, fourteen showed up the first time; and only two of those women have dropped out completely, even though they all do not come to every meeting.

So that first meeting took a great deal of work to set up. There simply is far more work involved in setting up a regional NETWORK, with no common professional bond among the members and no common workplace, than in creating a NETWORK within a corporation or existing professional group. At least four people have to be willing and able to commit large amounts of time, effort, and patience to this task, because the whole NETWORK is set up by word of mouth. The guiding philosophy of *bring-a-friend*, plus our decision to range as widely as possible in career fields, created a deliberately heterogeneous group. We set out to be exclusive, elitist, and clubby; we were determined to include only those women who were in accordance with our goals. And we came face to face with the fact that, sad to say, in one of the most populous, wealthy, and sophisticated areas in the United States, whole career paths were untrod by women.

Clubbiness

Perhaps we were fortunate in being willing to tackle the difficult problem of club spirit from the very first meeting. Any NETWORK operates on the principle of common bonding: the women involved, to lend each other mutual support, have to have something in common. In other words, we decided to have lunch only with women we wanted to have lunch with. This is a sticky point for any NETWORK. Women have been so brainwashed into being *nice* that it is extremely difficult to admit that we do not like someone. As one of us finally had the courage to say, "Look, I just don't want to meet with Ms. *ABC* for a monthly business lunch. She may be immensely successful; she may be professionally impeccable; she may even be useful to me. But I don't like being with her. She is too pushy, too aggressive, too abrasive for my tastes."

After one very trying and disruptive lunch meeting during which a hard-sell insurance agent had shown everyone pictures of her Mercedes with her name on her license plate, one network member said, "It's me or her. She gives me indigestion."

Although it took us many months, and a good deal of courage, to set up membership criteria and a structure for determining membership, we had decided on the most important fact even before the first meeting: we would *have* criteria, we would be selective, and we would ask the women we *chose* to join, and not issue blank invitations to all. We all agreed that we did not want to meet with women whom we felt could offer us little, and who, in addition, were personally unacceptable. When a NETWORK operates on a geographical basis, it has to attract members just as a men's club does. Being nice is not the point: creating a viable NETWORK of women who can and will help each other, is. We were able to work through our cultural conditioning and discard notions of niceness: our determination to stick to our goals helped us to eliminate guilt over those we left out.

From the start, our goal was to create a congenial club atmosphere where women of like mind, common interests, and similar levels of achievement could meet and NETWORK to help themselves and each other. To create that atmosphere, we needed not merely the right setting, but also the right kinds of women. We deliberately determined that the geographical NETWORK would be by invitation only, with that first telephone contact amounting to a virtual interview. The effort it took to create our list, issue the invitations, deal with responses, follow up the initial contacts, set up a mailing list, and keep track of all of the above was tremendous, especially in comparison with that of other networks with built-in means of communication, structure, and status identification. Fortunately, the rewards of effort and rigorous discernment were soon visible in our strong, well-integrated, and coherent group. We were clubby, yes, and it worked. Today we NETWORK even more closely and effectively than we did at the start. With a total of fifty women, in any one week we may NETWORK as follows: the banker and the stockbroker have a business lunch to discuss mutually advantageous ways of investing; the lawyers agree to run a symposium for single women at the dean's college; the dentist is asked for a referral to an orthodontist by the advertising manager; the surgeon writes a letter of recommendation to her medical school for the graphics firm owner's son. The networking runs exactly the way a club does: we all know each other, call each other, use each other, and see each other at least once a month. The work we did at that very first meeting, the preliminary decisions we made, has paid off in terms of lasting connections—networking.

The First Six Months
of Networking

CHAPTER FIVE

A TIME TO GROW

The first six months of any NETWORK resembles the cultivation of a garden of unknown seeds: the atmosphere has to be right for germination, but the end products are unknowable. When we replace the unknown hybrid seeds with humans, we have to concentrate on atmosphere. The most important task of the group in its infancy is the creation of an atmosphere that will allow a positive spirit to emerge. The worst thing that can happen in an early NETWORK is an overly rigid structure. There has to be room for experimentation, trial and error, hesitancy, and sporadic growth spurts as each group figures out what works best for it. Each group of women, whether within a corporation, a profession, or a geographical area, will cohere in a different way: women within corporations will be more conscious of male rejection by coworkers; women in professions will be more aggressive in career advancement; women in the same locale will be more, or less, elitist in accepting members. The group spirit varies tremendously, and the first requirement is that it be given room to grow. A deliberate characteristic of young networks should be tentativeness.

This idea of purposeful slowdown is very difficult to sell to women who have grown up with the women's movement, for they are aware that they are bucking the stereotype of the indecisive, unsure, wavering woman: the new networker feels it more desirable to be a nononsense, practical, decisive career woman. The echo of "Can't make up your mind? Just like a woman!" haunts us all. The negative image of 1960's consciousness raising groups as leaderless, vague, and disorganized anti-male gripe sessions, after which everyone went home and got divorced, must be countered. The prospect of setting up a consciousness raising model in the business arena is deplored by women who watched in frustration the fragmentation of those groups, the disintegration of a powerful women's movement, and the triumphant jeers of the maleocracy.

Though business women resist images of overly casual and disorganized semisocial ladies' groups, as well as the haunting specter of ineffectual and disruptive consciousness raising sisterhood, the new NETWORK must allow for at least six months' worth of informal meetings. These growth months should be exploratory, nonstructured, roundtable lunches with a group of women leading, rather than one strong president. This kind of informality is not in the least vague or disorganized; it is deliberately open-ended, leaving options for growth in as many directions as possible or necessary. It is a structure that emphasizes, not a particular direction for growth, but rather an atmosphere in which growth can take place. This is not consciousness raising by a long shot: no business or professional woman has time to waste in the middle of a day for a rap session. Networks whose luncheons become aimless forums for general antimale dissatisfaction quickly dissolve. The reason for such deterioration is not the method employed, but the unsuitability of the women involved for NETWORK formation. One research chemist explained to me that if she wanted to hear about male oppression, she could join her local golf club and gripe about "men only" times for weekend tee-offs. Working women seeking peer support are reaching for the strengths of those present, not playing victim to absent victimizers.

One reason this kind of reaching out takes time and careful deliberation is that networking involves women working together in new ways. This is all uncharted territory; prior to ten years ago there were insufficient numbers of women in significant positions in the work force for peer support to be a possibility. Only today, with ninety percent of women destined to work at some time during their lives, and a pitiful two percent in the top slots, are there enough *peers* to discuss mutual peer support! Because the phenomenon of women reaching for the top is so new, the very definitions of *peer support, career advancement,* and *educational outreach,* the three most commonly stated goals of networks, are open to discussion. At an early meeting of the New Jersey NETWORK, a woman banker exploded in anger and said, "Why should I travel one hour each way to hear a dozen women discuss what they're going to discuss?" I realized how new the concept of networks was, and how tentative it had to be. The psychiatrist in our midst said, with mild surprise, "You are really angry. Why? I bill at $50 an hour, and *I* think this is pretty interesting stuff being aired." The fears and hopes of each woman, as well as her expectations for this new enterprise of working together, proved fascinating and necessary to explore.

Women setting out to work together for mutual advancement have to feel comfortable with each other. The very casualness implicit in acquaintances that men take for granted is something quite new to women. Just as men are commonly acknowledged not to have "best friends," for that would be sissyish, women are not perceived as having "business buddies." Women are given social permission to have intense, personal, appearance-related friendships: any woman is expected to have a dressmaker, interior decorator, and hairdresser. How many women can have an accountant? Taking it one step further, how many times have you heard a career woman say, "My accountant is a genius. She devised the most innovative tax shelter I've seen." The whole concept of casual, business buddy relationships is so new to women that it has to be cultivated slowly and cautiously. Even the casual exchange of information is new and requires practice. Just as babies have to learn to talk, women in a NETWORK also must learn to talk in a special way, that mixture of shop and social talk that provides the backdrop for business contact-making. Perhaps even more to the point, women have to learn to listen to other women on a serious business level. A businessman commented to me that he never understood how women could do any business over lunch because they all talked at once and never ate: "I can't believe that these women do business together. No one listens to anyone else. I think they eat as little as possible just to talk as much as they can." He had an interesting point: men at business lunches do eat heartily, and while they're eating or drinking, they are also listening. Women, on the other hand, nibble on salads, leave half their food untouched, play with breadsticks, and dart in and out of conversations all during a meal. The art of *lunch*—a combination of deal-making, socializing, and eating—has to be relearned as women adapt themselves to the career world. This learning involves a group of women comfortable enough with each other to slow down and listen.

HONEST AND TRUE

In addition to learning about the business lunch, networkers must also set out two immediate ground rules: honesty and confidentiality. Several months of exploratory talks are needed to develop trust: each woman has to feel that nothing she says will leave the room, and that she will both give and receive honest appraisals, information, and advice. Honesty and confidentiality are needed for trust to grow, and that growth does not occur spontaneously. Because the concept of trust in the business world is so new to women, a realistic amount of time has to be allotted for its development. It takes a good deal of courage to feel comfortable enough with one's tablemates to request information or a favor. Women are afraid of appearing dumb, pushy, or naive. The level of ease has to evolve slowly before the intricate process of networking can begin. One young woman attorney who was working part time because of family commitments told me that it took her almost a year in a Women's Bar Association NETWORK to approach a government commissioner directly. She wanted some parttime work in labor law, but could not even ask for fear the commissioner would snub her. The power of an authoritative, experienced official was so terrifying that the young lawyer simply avoided the older woman until they had been to enough meetings together to establish eye contact and at least a nodding acquaintance. Finally, after almost a year, she was able to ask the question. As a happy ending, the commissioner was delighted to be able to help the younger woman, and is currently searching for parttime opportunities!

A Small World

The principle of confidentiality is necessary to all networks and has to be articulated openly. Each woman must feel confident that her input will not be repeated and that anything discussed within the NETWORK will remain private. Without this trust, neither genuine peer support nor real exchange of significant information will ever take place. Each corporation, profession, and geographical region is a small one; people have the oddest knack for knowing other people. Careless disclosure of confidences can and often does boomerang in the unlikeliest ways. Women who want to work together must be sure that these coincidences will not take place. A human resources specialist for a giant communications firm stressed the need for repeated assurances of confidentiality in a NETWORK. Her group formed two years ago and immediately set forth to discuss career problems. The only difficulty was, no one would talk. The first few meetings were characterized by chitchat, then silence. Finally she asked why the women were not more open. One psychologist replied, "How do I know that if I complain about my boss, and you switch jobs and end up with my company, you won't reveal my dissatisfactions to further your own career?" The group of women was shocked into an open discussion of the need to keep confidences within the NETWORK if anything was to be accomplished. Now the NETWORK is thriving; confidentiality is maintained by tight control over membership and insistence on absolute discretion by members. All industries are small worlds: one advertising manager told me that within a day everyone in the trade knew who appeared in the reception area of her firm if there was a job opening there.

The beginning networks have to stress repeatedly the need to keep confidences. At the very least, women must overcome the negative image of "loose tongues," and show themselves capable of keeping business secrets. Interestingly, women are beginning to perceive that *men* casually trade information far more readily than women do. Women networkers are only beginning to learn the lines of demarcation between genuine confidentiality and manic suspicion of everyone. Women know that the career world is a small one, but it takes months of working together to be sure that they can speak freely and not have everyone in town know what they said. If a NETWORK lunch becomes the next best thing to taking out an ad in the *Times*, the use of women by women will take on the kinds of sinister, manipulative overtones that unequal power situations give rise to. Confidence as a component of trust is a slow-growing creation.

Plain Talk

Along with a decision to keep the proceedings of the NETWORK confidential, there must also be a concomitant pledge of honesty. This also takes time to develop: women will not reveal themselves to other women merely by being thrown into the same room. Although women tend to be more open about feelings than men are, they are far less open about nonfeeling areas: the bottom-line career spheres of money, jobs, perks, and power. Since networks grow up as support systems for working women, honesty has to be transferred from the feelings area to that of so-called hard information. One of the most difficult areas for women to discuss openly is money; it takes a long time for women to feel comfortable enough with each other even to bring up the topic. I have never yet heard two women compare salaries in *dollar amounts* in public. Women who will reveal the most intimate details of their sex life, or the most revealing skeletons in the family closet, simply will not discuss dollars and cents with other women unless—and until—they are totally at ease with each other.

I have found that the hardest question for one woman to ask another is, "How much do you make?" There is a kind of taboo in discussing money that makes it truly the last frontier. In an era of openness, women still cannot discuss their salaries easily, openly, or comfortably. This wall of silence has undoubtedly been caused by great inequalities, still unremedied. Men have had the power of the purse strings, in the office as well as the home, and women have been afraid to ask for more for fear of losing all. When a sales manager in a construction machinery firm told me that she did not want to ask for an enormous salary increase, despite her distinct impression that she was paid at least forty percent less than men on line, she said: "I like this job; I like the company; I like the people. I really don't want to leave." The connection between her asking for an increase and being ordered to leave, as perhaps some kind of punishment for daring to ask, was painfully clear. This topic was discussed at length in an intracorporate NETWORK without a dollar sign ever being affixed to any woman's salary. To this day, money is discussed in only vague generalities. When will women in a NETWORK admit openly to their salaries? I don't know. But I do know that it takes months and months even to get around to the general topic of salary, let alone exact dollars and cents.

I NEVER DARED TO ASK

Perhaps the greatest difficulty women in careers have is daring to ask for higher salaries, more assistants, and lusher perks. In order to know what is a reasonable request, they need information which they have been taught not to ask for. Women can only gain access to the kinds of information men assume everyone knows if they can begin to ask about salaries, job descriptions, privileges, responsibilities, and chains of command. The rules of this game are not taught in schools; they are skills developed in the career mart and on the job. But women have not been in that world long enough to have developed asking skills; they have to make conscious decisions to NETWORK, to begin asking questions and comparing money and job information. The only leverage that women have is an ability to interrelate easily on a personal level; that marble has got to be the one used to transfer the interrelationships to career situations. Networks can be the vehicle for development of asking skills, but time has to be allowed for the personal relationships to mature sufficiently to allow nonpersonal questions to surface. Six months of networking may even be too little time for daring to ask or answer direct financial questions; it is certainly not too much time. I remember with glee sitting next to a dermatologist during a southern regional NETWORK meeting. A pension analyst commented that the New York Women's Bank had just turned the corner and made a profit: $60,000. The doctor turned to me and muttered, "Big deal. I make more than that in six months." I was delighted to hear, at last, the real scoop on what doctors did make. If she were making considerably less money—let us say the $12,000 that is the more usual female salary—she would probably not discuss any figure at all.

Perhaps it is only through networking that women will be able to compare notes about salaries, positions, and perks: certainly there have been few other channels for honest exchange of information in these areas. The lack of communication channels has, of course, prevented women's being paid what they were worth: if one functions in a vacuum, one has no idea of what salaries should be. Only recently have women become aware of using newspaper ads as guides to salary levels: a bookkeeper who returned to school to get a degree in accounting told a business and professional women's NETWORK group recently that for fifteen years she had been doing general accounting work while being paid bookkeeper's wages. She was so happy with her job—the boss, the office, the people, the flexible hours—that she never bothered to find out what the relationship between her work and her pay was. Of course she was shocked to discover that she could pass examinations in financial and managerial accounting without ever taking courses because she had been doing an accountant's job for years. When she decided that the time had come to leave her nest, and she began to read the ads, she was even more shocked to find that she should have been earning close to double her salary. She had deliberately come to this NETWORK meeting to share her experience with the other women.

Her honesty was extraordinary. Most often, women who begin to NETWORK take a good deal of time to develop the trust in each other that fosters honesty. There are far more compelling reasons to move slowly than to rush ahead in the first six months. The method of roundtable discussions, with informal leaders, is perfect for sharing of background information. The women have to get to know each other before they can begin to share information. While slow progress may cause a drop-off in attendance, rushing headlong towards goals not necessarily stated or approved by all can destroy the beginning NETWORK. The slower accretion of virtues not much discussed these days—honesty, confidentiality, trust, sharing—is the foundation of a successful, long-standing NETWORK.

WOMEN'S CORPORATE FEARS OF WOMEN

The first set of topics that an intracorporate NETWORK has to contend with are the fears associated with women gathering together. Of the three kinds of networks, the intracorporate one involves women most closely associated professionally and personally. One trait that has emerged in networking within a corporation is the amount of fear that accompanies women combining for peer support and mutual career advantage. The time to explore both the fears and hopes of corporate women is in the first months of the NETWORK. It is pointless to set up elaborate agendas, programs, membership activities, and criteria if the group is destined to founder on the rocks of suspicion, distrust, and negative attitudes. Several varieties of fear emerge in the relationships of women within corporations, and these fears should be articulated and fully explored at the first few meetings. In the course of this kind of activity, some women will drop out, and some may be added, but the end group will be a far more stable one than a NETWORK formed without mutual harmony. Because the risks within a corporation are greater than those in extracorporate networking, the fears of all the group members should be given air time. This may very well take up the bulk of the first few meetings: first the fears of all-woman groups have to be discussed, then the fears of male reactions to such groups. The group input is important to establish the notes of trust, confidence, and honesty that provide the connecting fluid that makes the NETWORK work.

The Queen Bee Syndrome

There will always be a handful of corporate women who have very specific, negative ideas about other women. Other working women are considered inferior, not worth associating with, and generally, second-class citizens. These women are the *queen bees*, corporate executives whose idea of equal opportunity is fifty young female file clerks led by an older female supervisor. Nothing whatever can be done about the queen bee's mindset; she is prejudiced against women and cannot be changed. Antifeminism, like anti-Semitism or antiliberalism, is almost impossible to remedy. The only positive action that can be taken by a group of networkers, whom of course the queen bee will not join, is ventilation of the problem. Only by discussing the syndrome can the networkers come to grips with this special breed.

To women who regard all women except themselves as inferior, the prospect of regular NETWORK luncheons will have no appeal whatever. A queen bee has already divided the world into three sexes—men, women, and herself. One NETWORK organized among line managers at a cosmetics company was spurned by a woman who, as marketing manager for a line of hair products on the East Coast, seemed a stellar role model for others. She refused to attend even the first session of an embryonic NETWORK, saying that the activity was far too feminist for her blood; she had no interest in an all-woman women's group. The NETWORK founders were at a loss: they had set up the group for line managers, and even before the first meeting, a classic example of the successful career executive had defected. At the first meeting, one founder brought up Manager X's absence. They discussed including staff women or perhaps inviting some junior members to replace the absent marketing manager. Finally, the most impatient and pragmatic woman said, "Let her go. Why must we have every woman here? Surely men's groups do not demand every line manager's presence. Stop taking attendance, and let's get on with what those of us who are here want to do."

The queen bee's fear of "all-woman women's groups" is a real one: a powerful hangover from the deep-seated feelings of competitiveness and inferiority women have about women. The NETWORK has to be willing to discuss the queen bee, and how to cope with her rejection of other women workers at her own rank. Early roundtable discussion of this syndrome will clear the air and enable the NETWORK to get on with the business of mutual support. The ability to deal with an upsetting topic, such as rejection, is more important than any push to corral all possible members, set up programs, or elect officers. When the NETWORK first begins, the act of sitting around a table and talking out the problems posed by a queen bee, as well as possible solutions, is a source of strength. If the NETWORK is to be viable the women who do not want to join as well as the women who do must be considered.

The Drone Syndrome

In addition to queen bees who refuse to join networks, the founders have to come to terms with women *they* choose to exclude: the *drones*. A real fear of corporate women is setting up criteria of exclusivity; they fear that they will offend peers or near peers by excluding them. Again, women have been socialized to think that it is not nice to leave someone out, especially when food is involved. Not sharing a luncheon is a little like relishing a glorious meal on the streets of Calcutta. The opposite of the queen bee syndrome is the drone syndrome, the urge to include all the women so that no one feels left out. This leads to ambivalence: acceptance of the *theory* of the need for exclusivity in networks, but reluctance to face the *reality* of someone's being left out. Some managers feel that women left out of a NETWORK will become their permanent enemies. No matter what the basis of organization for the NETWORK is to be, one soft-hearted executive will invariably say, "We can't leave Jane out." Jane is an executive secretary. Although the NETWORK consists exclusively of women vice presidents, someone will feel guilty about excluding Jane, arguing that Jane is far too intelligent for her present position, ambitious enough to want to rise into the managerial ranks, and capable of reaching the executive level. And the final argument, "Jane will feel awful if we don't include her," tells the real problem. The guilt here is enormous and must be talked out fully.

Even if rank lines are drawn with crystal clarity within a corporation, which they never are where women are concerned, the women networkers will have to exclude some women, unless they include *all* women, which is dangerous since it looks like unionization. The principle of exclusivity has to operate, not only because the appearance of unionization is undesirable, but also because the reality of women organizing on all ranks is not viable as a networking concept. The very idea behind this kind of group, peer support, clearly implies an organized arrangement of *peers*. But the guilt trailers, the fears of excluding nice, hard-working women who have not risen to certain levels, have to be discussed. The women who are in the NETWORK will have to consider their own feelings about those women who are left out. Since fears of excluding women on a professional basis represent a very new topic in the feminine psyche, these fears have to be discussed slowly and carefully. Again, roundtable exploration of members' views is the best way to handle women's reactions to being perceived as not nice by other women. If each networker contributes specific input, whether about women who are excluded, about her own exclusion from various groups, or about the sorority scenario, group sessions can deal with exclusivity fears. In time, networkers can feel comfortable with those left out as well as with their own "in" group.

We Talk Anyway

One other fear that corporate women have expressed is a nervousness that even peers feel about associating with each other on a formal, visible basis. Women often feel a specific desire not to organize with other women of their own rank, since, they say, a peer group is already functioning in an informal way. One editor in a large publishing company's NETWORK expressed this fear by saying, "Why bother to meet monthly, since we talk anyway and already know each other? What's there to gain by formality?" The hidden message is the desire to avoid open association with other women and simply to keep lines of communication going on a more covert basis, disguised as informality. The problem is one of *open* association with women, a fear that can have many causes, but the argument, *we talk anyway*, is one that is more amenable than most to discussion. When this objective is talked out, it almost always emerges that informal lines of communication get snafued. Like the children's game in which a word whispered into the ear of one person goes round a circle and comes out entirely different at the end of twenty repetitions, informal communications do not always work. In any group of women, if one is traveling, another is on vacation, and a third is changing her office, the message gets lost: a memo goes astray, a phone call is not received or returned, or an important interchange is postponed and never takes place. These contact systems are too fragile; formal networks are needed to correct this noncommuniction. The monthly meetings create a time and place for every woman to share input. Because women organizing professionally are so new a breed, some formal structure is needed.

Fear of this formal structure, this open meeting with other women, is a good topic for early discussion. The same editor who said that the women talked anyway was astounded to discover that, during her vacation, a major sales contest had been exposed by another editor as heavily weighted in favor of male sales executives. By the time she returned, discussion had died down, and the contest rules had already been changed: the tempest in the teapot was stilled. As another editor said, "This is what happens when we leave shop talk to chance; if we had monthly meetings, and round-robin topics thrown out, for sure sales contests would have been on the top of my list!" Corporate gossip? Maybe. But even if this sort of talk is gossipy, women have to air their fears of getting together to talk it. Why some women fear organizing to discuss mutual career concerns is a critical topic for networks to tackle early in their formation.

WOMEN'S CORPORATE FEARS OF MEN

Castration Complex

In addition to the fears corporate women have of other women peers' lunching together, and women are at a loss as to how to cope with this unwarranted fear, a further barrier to networking emerges from the close quarters in which everyone works. Even if *close* is defined as a fifty-story office tower or a sprawling suburban facility, somehow everyone knows what everyone else is doing. The power of corporate gossip never ceases to amaze working women; it is as if they imagine gossip will cease once they leave the backyard fence! Women executives who decide to meet on a regular basis fear three male reactions: ridicule, fear, and backlash. The spectacle of women lunching together for business purposes is still so new that all sorts of male reactions either occur, or are perceived to occur. What is clear is that the men never fail to notice women peers' lunching together, and women are at a loss as to how to cope with this unwarranted—and unwanted—attention. Since potential male reaction to women's groups is a deterrent to many women, these fears must be discussed at the outset.

Men's deep-seated fears of women's uniting lead to women's fears of uniting. This *is* a patriarchal society, especially in the business world, and any corporate woman who ignores that reality will not get very far. Woe unto the woman executive who refuses to admit to a fear of arousing male fear.

Men's fears of women are embedded in history, psychology, and sociology; they are the warp and woof of the human race, and perhaps beyond the scope of rational analysis. Much of men's panicky need to dominate women stems from these fears: men in the office feel that any disruption of the status quo will spread to the home as well. Womanpower represents the greatest modern threat to patriarchy; it is a new phenomenon in our society, at most a decade old. Men have no patterned way of reacting to women's sudden appearance in the executive suite; it is not even clear that men know that they have something new and probably permanent to react to. Corporate women are literally terrified to meet together because they know their male counterparts will feel a chill of fear at seeing women united for any reason whatever. This is not paranoia; it is common sense. As a woman auditor said, "If the only two women executives in the accounting department happened to get on the same elevator together every day, within a week the men would have invented a plot for us to be hatching." She added that the two women consciously went out of their way to avoid each other during working hours just to quiet fears of an impending revolution.

Women must work at understanding the automatic male fears triggered by any group of women meeting together. An early series of NETWORK discussions could be an examination of these male fears and female reactions to them. The men react automatically, and with hostility. It does no good for women to ignore the fears, play to them by being deliberately abrasive, or cower in corners. All of these defensive reactions must be replaced by honest, open, direct contact-making in networks. In order to defuse some of the hostility and clear the air of rancor, the beginning NETWORK has to encourage discussion of male fears. Women's studies provide a good background for the new ideas which have inspired women and frightened men. In working with an intracorporate NETWORK I found that a program of historical, sociological, and linguistic background was useful in getting women to understand where men were coming from. If the point of networking is support and advancement, no woman can afford to forget that she is trying to be upwardly mobile in a man's world. The NETWORK can help by dealing with the kinds of fears prevailing in that world which can either combine to hold the woman down, or be used in her behalf. The networks destined to succeed and genuinely help the women involved will be those that operate with knowledge, clear sightedness, and understanding of men and their weaknesses.

THE JOKE'S ON US

The early NETWORK must deal with women's fear of male ridicule. Perhaps this ridicule is men's response to their own fear, a kind of nervous laughter in the face of the threat of women united. Such institutionalized nastiness is a perfectly predictable reaction. Again, women have to examine their own reactions to male ridicule so that they are not immobilized by it. When men see women lunching together, or even walking and chatting together in the office, they often feel obligated to make remarks about "hen parties" or "girl talk," even if the women are senior partners. There is an intense need to belittle the women by trivializing them. As a result, women who want to get together and form a NETWORK fear being considered silly, and men play to this fear. One two-hour meeting of an executive women's group devoted to a searching analysis of the budget for the upcoming year, dispersed, only to be greeted by the nearest male executive's comment: "Deciding to redecorate the cafeteria again?" The entire process of budget analysis, a corporate experiment to isolate the women executives' input, exploded in a rash of ill-feeling at this condescending reaction.

But the woman manager must remember that underneath the giggle is man's deep fear of women combining. If one woman represents a threat to office morals and manners, and even to the home front, how much more of a threat is a unified, serious, committed group? Such a group could easily take over a corporation. And it is exactly that fear of women *teaming up* in networks that surfaces as male ridicule. For the women who are embarrassed by male snipings at "hen parties"—and it is this sensitivity that men use to manipulate women into *not* working together—a healthy talking out session is needed. The women's fears of male ridicule must be examined: Why is it so devastating to be accused of "girl talk"? Women's fears on this score have to be discussed early on in NETWORK formation to prevent the loss of women who would be more intimidated by ridicule than by overt hostility. Because women have had such difficulty in being taken seriously as dedicated career people, ridicule is the sharpest weapon a male colleague has. Most people can handle nastiness far better than they handle mockery; in our society we lose face when we are laughed at. A woman who has worked years for her success can be undone, not by business errors or by male refusal to communicate with her, but by laughter. In the male arsenal, laughter is the best weapon. One of the saddest humiliations the woman executive promoted from the secretarial ranks has to endure is the never-ending stream of snide comments about "leaving her typewriter behind," "getting a man secretary," and "polishing her nails while she *gives* dictation."

The need to discuss women's shrinking reaction to male ridicule is urgent; it is a primary task of the forming NETWORK. For women to keep a low profile means that they will hug the floor indefinitely, especially without each other's help, if they refuse to discuss their own fears openly. Perhaps the very impetus to form networks represents a healthy trend toward examining women's feelings about the men they work with. In any case, since more than two women represent a serious threat to male dominance, the NETWORK must prepare members for possible male reactions. One woman who is the highest placed officer in an investment banking firm, a rare bird on Wall Street indeed, told me that she used to have nightmares about falling down the two steps leading to the executive dining room. Her nightmare was not about breaking her ankle: she was afraid that the all-male diners would laugh. Such fears put women executives under added stress; through networks, these fears can be discussed and alleviated.

MALE BACKLASH

Another fear women have is the fear of a male backlash against uppity women organizers. Women who think that their male peers "include me anyway" are quick to point out that the men may cease to include them if the women begin associating together. It is as if in the game of status, the real reward, a lunch date with the men, will be taken away if the women dare to go out with each other. It is reminiscent of the 1950s ethic, when going out with the girls meant that you had lost the main prize, a date with a man. Women lunching with women is viewed as last prize, while women dining with men becomes the golden ring of victory. The carryover from the sexual competition for a real golden circle, a wedding band, is part and parcel of the 1950s inheritance, as well as a reflection on true corporate power structure. But the feelings that women have about their own inferiority must be openly examined. If women articulate the fear that the organization of a NETWORK will somehow remove them from eligibility to lunch with men, the exact reasoning behind this has to be explored. This fear reflects the belief that the real power structure is male: the female NETWORK is merely ersatz. If that feeling is not expressed and dissipated, women will never come to see themselves as first-class citizens entitled to inhabit the marketplace.

After all, it is just possible that in the future men will want to be included in women's groups. In one corporate NETWORK, marked by wholehearted management commitment from the chairman of the board down, the women emerge from each luncheon so enthusiastic and energetic that the men have been spotted hovering outside the board room, almost appearing to listen in. No man has yet approached a woman manager to *ask* for an invitation, but the women networkers know that they are being watched in a positive way. The men sense a positive kind of womanpower and want to work with it. They have a great many fears, they often say precisely the wrong things to the women, but they are curious enough to make the women suspect that they want to move into that NETWORK. Perhaps this is an isolated case, but I cannot help thinking that corporate men want to communicate with corporate women, and vice versa. The problem is that in this age of transition, no one is precisely sure how to do it. The old vocabulary for male boss and female secretary is no longer usable; a new vocabulary for male executive and female peer has not been invented yet.

While we are in this age of transition, the formation of a NETWORK is an important step that women can take to support each other in an often hostile career world. This networking, in summary, has to proceed very slowly and with caution: it is an experiment, with the results as yet unknown. Women's fears of each other and of men must be set out on the table and thoroughly explored before other questions come up. The atmosphere of trust, honesty, and confidentiality has to be established before the networking can begin in earnest. Networking is a delicate process, almost like weaving a thin web of connection among disparate elements. The web must be woven carefully and slowly for it to be strong enough to last.

The future undoubtedly holds the promise of coed networks. As men and women become more accustomed to working with each other, the common bonds in the workplace will eradicate gender differences. Although I feel that coed networking will occur in the long run, the long run is rather a distance away. For the time being, the most successful networks operate as either all-male or all-female. I look forward to the day when networking transcends gender, but in view of the fears articulated by women forming networks at present, the New Woman networks have a way to go before they can combine with the Old Boy ones.

Structuring the
NETWORK

CHAPTER SIX

During the first few months of networking, little organizational discussion takes place. The excitement is generated by communal talk about interconnected fears, hopes, career goals, sharing, and mutual support. This is a time of feeling-out, a time when what the women do, basically, is decide whether or not they have anything in common. In the simplest possible expression of a complex set of motives, the NETWORK group has to decide if it can cohere: Do the women *like* each other? Contrary to popular opinion, there is no such thing as "like at first sight." There is a period of time during which the NETWORK members are quite wary of each other: trust, sharing, and confidence take time to build. During this six months or so, there is little point in building an elaborate structure; after this time, however, efforts must be made to build an organization in order to prevent the kind of dispersal of momentum that can wreck the NETWORK.

Interestingly, the timing is less of a problem in practice than in theory: women in a group sense when the time has come to consider matters like dues, agendas, minutes, and budgets. I have found that after six months of regular meetings, one member of any NETWORK will simply decide to take notes; those notes become the minutes, and a formalized structure can begin. In the case of New Jersey NETWORK, a very quiet investment analyst, whom we all thought of as a numbers person, showed up with a full set of minutes after we had been meeting for close to a calendar year. She announced that we were drifting, and read to us exactly how vague our last meeting had been. She was quite right, and we did go on to build an organization, for none of us wanted to end up, as one member put it, "discussing toenail polish and hemlines."

MEASURING WITHOUT A RULER

Before this structure grows out of the group, the indefinable process of measuring the intangible—the "like" quotient among the members—has to take place. Like a good stew, the varied ingredients have to be allowed to simmer undisturbed for a period of time. The women in the NETWORK have to take each other's measure; they have to find out if each wants the same things in terms of careers, lifestyles, and commitments. They need to explore similarities in background, aspirations, and levels of achievement. There is a clubby atmosphere being built; like all club spirit, it is built on intangibles. The real question in each woman's mind at the first NETWORK meetings is, "Is the woman next to me one of us? Is she on my wavelength? Does she want my support as a peer? Are we really peers?" The early answers are nonanswers: "wait and see," "be patient," "let it flow." Fortunately women can afford patience: the myth of the indecisive female can be used to advantage. There is no reason to feel pressured into deciding whether or not a woman networker is *one of us* until enough time has passed to get to know her.

One of the reasons that time is necessary is that women have always measured the tangible in other women. The intangibles of professional life, such as attitudes towards power, feelings about career commitments, and honest desire to make money are things which women are entirely unaccustomed to sniffing out in other women. Visible status can be measured easily by Puccis and Guccis. To women who wish to NETWORK and form their own power base, the fine art of judging other women is in its infancy. The old rules have to be thrown out: women in networks are making judgments about each other in distinctly nonsexual, noncompetitive ways. A NETWORK woman may dress all wrong: polyester Polly in a sea of Molloy navy flannel. A woman can sound all wrong: a New York accent amidst clipped *seven sisters* speech. A woman can be married, or unmarried, all wrong: a postal clerk husband lurking in a group of investment bankers, or a discreetly gay woman among straights. Still, the NETWORK *one of us* decision is not based on any of the above factors. The wrong style of dress, accent, husband, or sexual persuasion can all be irrelevant if the NETWORK member is one of the career elite: a dedicated, success-oriented, and power-prone, probably Type A professionally committed woman. The most successful career woman in one NETWORK wears unmatched separates, has chipped nail polish, drinks too much, smokes too much, and is personally abrasive to boot. She is also the single most powerful woman in management in her industry. In spite of the fact that this executive looks and sounds nothing like the rest of her NETWORK members, it is readily apparent from what she says, the authority and expertise with which she conveys her message, that she is not only *one of us* but probably the standard-bearer for all the rest.

Time is needed for the NETWORK to jell because snap decisions made on the basis of clothing, speech patterns, and manners may very well be inaccurate: the women networking, especially if they are in different age groups, have to leave a wide swath for differences caused by changing times and mores.

In the early meetings, before a specific structure emerges, there is a kind of informal, leaderless, round-table discussion. The women talk among themselves, but the early organizational thrust should be to start a pattern of introductions by each member. One of the founders generally suggests that each person introduce herself briefly; the next step is to go around the table, or tables, and have all the women make these introductions. The three kinds of networks all need this structuring; even within a corporation, the women executives will be visible to each other, but not necessarily known. In a professional or regional NETWORK group, the women are not known to each other at all and have to set up some means of communication. The roundtable format is comfortable for almost everyone: even the painfully shy can speak their piece without being put on the spot in any way. The briefest introduction I've ever heard was given by a woman doctor whom everyone thought rather cold; it took us two years to realize that she was extremely shy. At our first few meetings she would simply say, "I'm XYZ. I'm a radiologist." She would then turn hopefully to the woman next to her, indicating that her own introduction had ended!

SHOW AND TELL

Even the most recalcitrant NETWORK member will participate in a roundtable exchange of information, which I call "show and tell," and which is the basic activity that occupies the first six months or so of networking. This show and tell is the first concrete task of a NETWORK, and is a method of clarifying each member's professional sphere. Show and tell comes to mind because there is an almost childlike fascination in every career woman about what other successful women do, and how they got to the point of doing it. This curiosity is almost never verbalized because it sounds so silly: How can grown women, professionals all, be so unaware of what other professionals really do? But if we stop to think about it, how can we *not* be unaware? We have no lawyers, bankers, or accountants to chat with at the golf club. In fact, we have no golf club. We have no real career counseling to fall back on; anyone over thirty probably never received hard career information in terms of exactly what women did all day in jobs other than nursing or teaching. So most women are in the dark about what career executives and professionals do. Even women within the same corporate NETWORK cannot be assumed to know the precise job functions of their peers in different areas. How often have we heard, "What is it that you folks in advertising *do* all day?" This lack of information is not at all astonishing if we think of how few women have been trained in business schools in the past, and the complexity of modern business. In addition to the lack of business training, most women in corporate slots have become so specialized in the course of their career paths that they have never mastered the organizational charts. Even professionals in the same general sphere, doctors for instance, are dealing with such a burgeoning amount of specialization that it is necessary for a specialist in one area to explain her job to someone in another field.

And so, a very legitimate first activity in any kind of NETWORK is a sharing of information about each woman's professional sphere and background. Women are eager to share with other women information about what each one does; even the shyer ones can be persuaded, given time, to open up. Eventually, when she feels comfortable in the group, Dr. XYZ will discuss how she came to choose radiology as a field, what she does with her days, what kinds of satisfactions she gains, and what kinds of problems she has. The early forms of introduction can eventually be expanded from roundtable and random impromptu speeches to more formalized activity. But the beginning process of any NETWORK is a mutual sharing of input by each person present, to the extent she feels able to speak before a group. Everyone says something, even if the introduction is minimal.

WHERE DID YOU GO? OUT.
WHAT DID YOU DO? NOTHING.

The short introductions are fascinating because one topic of consuming interest is what women in industry, the professions, and the academic world *do* all day long. The stockbroker wants to know what the anesthesiologist does; the advertising account executive wants to know what the labor lawyer does; the dentist wants to know what the television producer does. Even though all of these women probably feel that what they do is so simple that the others will laugh at detailed explanations, the others are usually fascinated. While women have been ridiculed for discussing the fine points of floor wax or hemlines, and so may fear giving detailed explanations of anything, the topics of what you *do* in most any career is as yet new ground to cover. Women giving the introductions have to get over the fear of being boring. To women relatively new to the work force, and babes in the executive woods, this topic is endlessly interesting. The dentist in a regional NETWORK told me that she felt quite inadequate in such a creative group: all she did, she thought, was skilled, mechanical labor, which she considered quite routine. To the other networkers, the arts of root canal and oral surgery seemed highly creative, not at all routine tasks; the other women thought that their jobs palled in comparison. This glamour on the other side of the fence provides months of fascinating discussion, since what highly paid, highly trained people do is neither all dull nor all exotic. Women, especially, have to explain every step of their way, and they always have an appreciative audience in other women.

The format for the first six months of informal introductions is a natural kind of roundtable sharing among NETWORK members: each woman introduces herself briefly. The introduction can include not only her present position and its functions, but also a brief description of her background, education, previous career history, and other interests or family situation. When a NETWORK has a constant number of members, as intracorporate networks generally do, or when the group is small, this process takes a minimal amount of time per meeting and just a few months worth of meetings to accomplish. In regional networks, however, or even professional women's groups where more than a dozen or so women are involved, the roundtable format can be endless, and eventually repetitive. In the New Jersey NETWORK, because different members showed up each time, we were in danger of introducing and reintroducing ourselves for a decade. After close to a year of this, we realized that we had to move on to a more satisfying structure.

The most satisfactory and smooth transition from roundtable introductions to more structured organization for networks is the creation of panels to answer the question, "And what do you do?" In all three types of networks, the second six months of life can deal with members' presentations of job-related information in panel forums. The structure of the panel is excellent for putting members at ease: if three or four women have presentations, no one person is forced to speak at great length. And if someone cannot get to the meeting, the group is not left hanging. A natural second step following the individual introductions is using the group members as resource people. This kind of explanatory activity meets a constant need of the members, because of the curiosity about what each one is doing. It has the extra advantage of being free, before budgets are set up, as well as interesting. The panel presentation of personal experience works out extremely well for all three types of NETWORK, although it has to be tailored to each.

THE CORPORATE DAY

Women in corporations are detail-oriented, precise, and factual to a greater degree than even they think; all it takes, often, is comparing notes in a NETWORK to determine how efficient the female corporate executive is. In an intracorporate NETWORK, the formalized kind of introduction can be used as a very effective tool for the female manager on her upwardly mobile path. If each networker is assigned the activity of making a presentation to the others of "A day in the Life of . . ." she can be told that a useful aid to memory is a diary or calendar log. If she has a month in which to prepare, she can keep track of her time and functions so that she can present an accurate picture of her job responsibilities to the others. This log can then become an extremely valuable tool in the individual woman's career track: when asking for a raise, a promotion, or a new assistant, it is always useful to have *exact* information about tasks done, time spent on each, preparation, and "at-home" work.

In one intracorporate NETWORK, the personnel manager explained her job by taking an imaginary new employee, Leslie Doe, through that employee's first day on the job. The personnel manager logged her own day side by side with Leslie Doe's, and explained her tasks in terms of what she had to do for new employees. She then added extra details about her own work not related to new employees, and, in effect, gave a short course in personnel to the rest of her corporate associates. The other corporate women were all ears: they were astonished to hear the kinds of tasks a non-line manager performed, tasks they had not thought about in years. One sales representative said, "I never realized how much was involved in your sector; I've really only thought of personnel as the place I send my doctor bills to, and then send my complaints when I fail to get a refund!" The personnel manager grinned, and said, "Keep up your end in sales and maybe we'll be able to afford a more generous medical plan."

The lack of spontaneous interchange of information even within a corporation is highlighted by the avid interest each woman shows in the job of the other. Because women in business have not felt free to consult each other and have not had the men's room as a consultation center, informal interchanges which men consider routine never take place. It is only at the NETWORK luncheons that some of this becomes apparent. Often women within corporations are simply afraid to ask their peers what each one does; they fear appearing foolish or intrusive. While men can casually chat on the way to the water cooler, dealing information such as "Well, what's doing in your shop? How are bonds these days?"—women have had no practice in this kind of exchange. It takes formal presentations, in a regularly constituted group organization, for an individual corporate woman to come to an understanding of what the others outside her department are doing. To the extent that women have to become generalists, rather than specialists, to rise in the corporate world, this kind of informational dealing is crucial. One corporate woman, a real-estate attorney in a large brokerage house, told me that before a NETWORK was formed, she was totally insulated not only in her own office, but also within her own department. She never knew who to ask questions about the general business of securities sales, so she simply stuck to her own tasks. She summed up a very typical attitude of corporate women when she said, "I could have worked in that building for twenty years, knowing everything not only about our building, but the other properties as well, and without understanding the transactions that generate the money to pay for these properties." Without the NETWORK group, she would have remained comfortably with her clauses and paragraphs, never bothering to inquire into the nuts and bolts of her corporation.

The corporate day is an excellent way for intracorporate women to present themselves to their peers: the topic is at hand, the information is right there, and the gathering of it in log form can have many extra benefits. If each woman has to make a fifteen-minute presentation of her day to the others, she will not only clarify her job duties in her own head, but also enlighten her fellow networkers. At least two such presentations can be made per meeting; and the discussions following will undoubtedly generate fascinating questions and a good deal of personal sharing. One presentation I witnessed by a coding manager in a bank's head office led to a discussion of corporate women and travel: the coding manager had made a trip to a regional office to examine a new computer system. Her major anxieties dealt not with the new system, but with the actual trip. As a result of her presentation, the discussion veered off into what the regional offices were doing, and then into the area of women on business trips. A decision was made to schedule an entire

NETWORK luncheon about "Women and Business Travel," since that topic loomed high on the stress index for all the executives present. The show and tell approach can work itself out into topics for future discussion, programs to be planned for upcoming meetings, and outside speakers to be selected for the group. The momentum begins, however, with in-group sharing of information.

WHITHER BAKKE?

The need for show and tell, in the form of a panel of two or more speakers, exists in professional women's groups as well as intracorporate networks. The panel format is particularly well-suited to this kind of group, because the number of NETWORK members will undoubtedly be larger than a dozen at the first meetings: an announcement of a group to be formed, appearing in a journal or bulletin that already circulates widely, will draw more members than an intracorporate NETWORK, where out of even a thousand managers, no more than twenty will likely be women! In professional women's groups, there are already large numbers of women in law, and growing numbers in medical fields: ten percent of all physicians are women, a far larger share than the two percent figure for corporate executives. The major advantage for women who wish to NETWORK and who already are members of professional groups is the communication system of the existing group: neither the corporation nor the region has that built-in factor. Thus, the women's group from one profession or one branch of the academic world can count on a larger number of responses to the initial bid for networking.

Because there will be more women attending the first meeting, setting up panels of four to five women will be workable. The topics to be considered should be almost purely practical, show and tell in the same concrete sense that intracorporate presentations were. Within a profession, the panelists will want to deal with choices that women must make after they have chosen law, medicine, teaching, and so forth. At the New York Women's Bar Association NETWORK meeting, topics of interest to everyone were the following:

1. "Dual Careers in the Same Office: Can a Husband and Wife Partnership Survive in the Home and the Office?"
2. "The Juggling Act: Career, Husband, Home, Children"
3. "Choosing between Private Practice, an Established Law Firm, and a Corporate Legal Department"
4. "Overt and Covert Sexism: Male Attitudes towards Women Lawyers"
5. "Future of Law: When Half the Lawyers Are Women"

In the Bar Association's NETWORK, there were enough lawyers in each of the categories—private practice, large law firms, in-house counsel, husband and wife teams, small law firms—to form panels to provide the kind of sharing the group wanted.

Another advantage of the panel format is that it can avoid duplication of efforts by the speakers. The four or five women in the same area of their profession can have a preliminary meeting to discuss the kinds of things each wants to say about her career, including whether or not she chose the career, or it chose her! I was curious whether this kind of information was necessary. As a non-lawyer, I assumed that the question of career choice had been discussed to death in law school, either through practical seminars for the students, career counseling services, or outside speakers. One recent graduate of a prestigious law school enlightened me. She said that career counseling at her alma mater consisted of a crusty old male professor's saying, "Since you're taking up a seat here, I suppose you'll work for a while. But you'll get married and have children, so why don't you take something or other with a government department, and leave the big jobs alone?" I was shocked to hear the same lines I had heard in graduate school fifteen years ago; things may be changing, but there are enough relics around to make a women's NETWORK essential for career advancement. The real information was never given to the women lawyers I spoke to: they were not counseled in law school about career paths, salaries, partnerships, firms which discriminated against women openly or subtly, or fields of law hostile to women. They were never told that in certain courts, such as family court, which are populated by what one lawyer called, "housewife-cum-lawyer types," women attorneys are almost automatically viewed as dilettantes. One young lawyer summed up the need for exchange of useful information about careers when she said, "All the law school seminars that deal with the outside world are called, 'Whither Bakke? The Future of Antidiscrimination Legislation.' What I need to be told are things like what is the address of the housing court, and where is the nearest parking lot."

There is apparently a need for women already in professions to share common experiences and tales of life in the real business world: the things law school, medical school, dental school, and business school never taught you. These are locker-room sorts of topics; they deal with reality—money, fees, advancement, logistics, and attitudes. These topics revolve around sharing information from diverse sources to which women have not had access until now. In some cases, input from a banker, a broker, a candlestick maker would also be helpful; but since when have women had friends like this? There have been no buddies for women to ask about kinds of law practice, or even details of daily life in court. The lawyer out on her own, whether she is in her own practice, a law firm, or a corporation, has had no one to ask for advice, share problems with, or help her over the small but stressful hurdles of daily life. The kinds of panels set up to deal with exactly these questions could be a great service performed by the NETWORK. "Whither Bakke?" has to be supplemented by what women are supposed to do in the decades before they get to argue cases in Supreme Court. The NETWORK input can be tremendously helpful, because there are always the fears women have of looking foolish by asking obvious questions and evoking male laughter. The fear is the same whether the woman is a corporate executive or a practicing attorney; women do not want to expose themselves to ridicule. An all-female NETWORK of like-minded women, who have declared themselves ready to help each other, is supportive, nonthreatening, and highly informative on a practical level. The panels set up by groups of women in professional networks can be a remarkably beneficial way to organize at least six months worth of meetings. After these panels have been held, one professional group can certainly have a clearer feel for what is needed in outreach to others. Once the NETWORK has mined its own resources, the steps beyond are easier to take.

TELL ME A STORY

In the case of regional networks, the show and tell approach to organizing meetings is an exciting venture for all: The diversity within the group is so great that each woman's success story is new and different from the one before and the one after. While it is neither kind nor practical to request one woman to tell her story to the group for an entire meeting, no more than two women in similar fields should be scheduled for the same date. Each speaker is requested to tell her story to the group: what she does, how she got to do it, what kinds of problems she has faced or still faces. No more than two stories can be dealt with per luncheon; the tales are so fascinating that numerous questions arise. The listeners, all of whom represent different areas of career achievement, generally deluge the speakers with questions; the excitement in hearing true career success stories is enormous because the group is so very diverse. Each woman is eager to hear how the other one made it. These are all success stories, remember, and nothing appeals to these audiences more than real-life tales of upwardly mobile women. The first story in the New Jersey NETWORK was told by a newspaper editor who had risen to her present position, editing a daily section of a major metropolitan newspaper, without so much as a college degree! In addition, she had raised four children, was and is happily married to her original spouse, and had been employed throughout her entire marriage. She began in the clippings room and rose through the ranks to her present position. After she told her story, she presented a problem she faces on the job today: Should she accept a hefty raise in pay, with no new title, or hold out for a promotion in rank as well as money? The risk was that a younger man had been promised the new title at a lower salary; she might forfeit both the money and the job. Needless to say, our NETWORK did not come up with a clearcut happy ending, but we did have an extraordinarily interesting lunch session discussing this woman's past career experience and current dilemma.

Story after story captivates regional NETWORK members because each one is so different. The success story of women in careers, a new phenomenon, is composed of unique tales told by women with certain qualities in common: dedication, professionalism, and competence. The personalities differ, but the success traits in elite networkers surface as a common denominator. Another common denominator in most networks is that the road to the top—as measured by salary, prestige, power—is rarely straight. Many women in networks have undergone career switches, often from traditional careers, especially teaching, to nontraditional ones, such as dentistry, labor law, or engineering. Those who did not detour to law, medicine, or advertising via teaching often made career detours via marriage and childbearing: when their children were older, instead of turning to Bloomingdale's or the country club, the women decided to make a career commitment. Only a small percentage of the successful women I have met in networks, mostly those under thirty-five, in fact, actually began in one profession and progressed in a straight line through career as well as marriage, children, and homemaking. The true stories illustrated some unusual patterns, but no conclusions can be drawn at this stage about the dual career family, since each one is unique.

One similarity that did emerge in the year of stories told by my New Jersey NETWORK was that the successful dual career families involved men and women in the same profession, but different branches of it. One husband and wife medical family includes a male psychiatrist and a female allergist; one corporate family involves a male investment banker and a female financial analyst. A teacher-lawyer family is interesting because it includes a female lawyer who had been a teacher before she went to law school; she had taught reading, while her husband, a mathematician, had veered off into administration as math department head in his college. While conclusions are not possible about the meaning of this data, since each dual career family is unique, the stories are the fun part. The successes, detours, and compromises of the members all occupied the better part of a year for the New Jersey NETWORK. There were, in fact, luncheon meetings where the second speaker never got the chance to discuss herself fully: too many questions were put to the first speaker to leave sufficient time. One of the most exciting stories, told by the woman dentist, was her career decision: She had been a science teacher and decided to pursue a career in dentistry when she was over thirty. She received no encouragement whatever from anyone: family, dental college professors, or fellow students. In fact, she still recalls being pointedly addressed as "Mrs. *ABC*," when everyone else, except for the requisite two young women students, was "Mr." Still she kept at it, borrowing money to stay afloat, surviving a divorce and parental disapproval. She ended her story by saying, "And now I have two young male dentists working for me!" Our NETWORK applauded.

So the stories told by each speaker represented a source of fascinating information for many months. In each type of NETWORK, this is the case: the inner resources of the group can be used to structure the meetings for at least a year. Networks within a corporation, a professional women's group, or a geographic region all have sufficiently varied input to enable fruitful interactions to take place. The formalized structure of presentations by individuals or panels enables the members to get to know each other in the course of time. The self-introductions form a perfect way of determining the common bonds, in addition to providing learning experiences for all. But there is the danger of monotony—a kind of group NETWORK burn out—if a greater degree of organization is not put into effect in about a year. At a certain point, the change from profitable interaction to stagnation becomes evident. At this point a firmer step towards organization must be taken.

GETTING THE ACT TOGETHER

The act of formal organization, far from being a threatening one, is a series of more or less routine steps for any woman who has belonged to an organization. The NETWORK needs dues, directors, agendas, a budget, and membership criteria. The last is sticky, and a point to be considered elsewhere, but the other paraphernalia of structure can be handled at one meeting. The leaderless roundtable gives way to a sort of institutionalization, and those procedures are somewhat routine. The novelty in networking is the philosophical substructure, the personal interplay and sharing on a professional level; the structure of the organization turns out to be similar to most structures, and not too problematical except for membership criteria. Our NETWORK in New Jersey became structured once we saw the minutes and realized that we were becoming aimless. As a regional group, we were in danger of becoming an endless show and tell society, and the viewing of our proceedings on paper was proof that we were indeed drifting.

Before that point arrives, there are certain steps to be taken in creating a structure. The act cannot be gotten together for free, so the first step is establishing dues. This step holds true for any type of NETWORK: a financial base must be created in the form of a bank account. Money is needed for mailing announcements, printing costs or advertising costs for those announcements, secretarial help, room rentals, and speaker fees. A minimal dues fee is ten dollars per member, but twenty-five dollars is more realistic; that provides enough in the bank for the publicity and ancillary items such as rooms, beverages, and speakers. Once money is collected, there must be a treasurer and a bank account. The dues are generally payable for a year, and it is simplest to use the calendar year, giving everyone a grace period until January 1 to join. The most complicated and least purposeful method is the individual twelve-month period for all members, beginning with the date each person joins. Until the NETWORK decides to buy a club, there is little point in such complex bookkeeping. A bank account is a good idea, and eventual incorporation may be considered as well.

After dues are instituted, a treasurer on duty, and a bank account set up, the next step is selection of officers. A NETWORK needs a secretary to take minutes, a secretary to supervise sending out announcements and other correspondence, and two or three directors. No formal organizational chart is needed if no one wants it; the group will function, like all groups, on a committee base, and the degree of title-granting can conform to the comfort level of the women networkers. No nonprofit NETWORK that I have run into has a full slate of officers: the organization is remarkably informal in all types of groups. Still, for career advancement purposes, a board of directors is a good idea, since the entry looks good on a resume: "Board of Directors, New York NETWORK." While women seem quite able to do without heavy structure, we have to be careful not to downplay our abilities and efforts.

OH, IT WAS NOTHING

Due to women's tendency to say, when confronted by a compliment on anything from a lovely meal to successful surgery, "Oh, it was nothing," the NETWORK board of directors should be clearly published as a structure. The names ought to be listed on the letterhead, with one director on top. There has been some resistance to that idea, because it smacks of the patriarchal society, military modes, and corporate structures women are left out of. Women tend to move towards egalitarian kinds of organization. Many times I have heard the comment, "But we don't need a director or anything that formal." While this may be true, networks do need a director, a board, secretaries, and a treasurer for the sake of the women doing the work. Any woman in a NETWORK who does organizational work without pay should be rewarded by a nice title for her resume. I almost fell into the *Oh, it was nothing* trap: Having done all the publicity for my own NETWORK, and all the writing as well, I finally decided to claim the title of public relations director. It helped a great deal when I was job hunting to produce written press releases and newspaper articles that my efforts had garnered. Over-modesty is foolish; if we have a better mousetrap, who will know it without advertising?

The routine work will then be annual collection of dues, disbursement of monies, taking and sending of minutes if desired, and sending out announcements of meetings. *Every* meeting must be preceded by a written reminder. This is the job of the corresponding secretary. Whether the form be interoffice memo, announcement in a bulletin, or direct mail, each monthly meeting must be publicized to each member. Word of mouth will not do! A helpful aid is an annual calendar of meetings, distributed in September or January, but as a supplement, monthly notices are still needed. NETWORK women are not forgetful; they are just busy. In the New Jersey NETWORK, after our major organizational meeting, the stockbroker heaved a sigh of relief and said, "Well, that's done! Now we are all big girls, and we don't have to be reminded that we meet

on the second Thursday of the month. See you in August."
Needless to say, on August 8, exactly three women
showed up. We three decided, without any major votes,
that we had to reinstate the monthly notices.

The Committee to Create Committees

The last organizational chore is the creation of
committees. The directors generally function as heads,
and each one works best with three or four women. There
is normally a committee on programs, one on luncheon
planning, and, as we shall see, a committee for the directory. The publicity, finances, and recordkeeping and correspondence departments each can be handled by one
person. And there is a committee on membership, which
has some fairly crucial tasks at the outset. When needed,
of course, other committees can be formed. The advantage of this structure is flexibility and an *ad hoc* ability to
react to new developments. The old adage, "when in
doubt, form a committee," works well, because the concept of women networking is so new that early decision-
making is best done by a few heads working together,
rather than by fiat. One committee chairperson in an intracorporate NETWORK told me that she had assumed the
responsibility for setting up the luncheons, since she is
something of a gourmet, and the group meets in the Wall
Street area, not exactly a foodlover's paradise. All went
well until she decided that a new Indian restaurant would
be a novel treat: several burned palates later, she decided
that in the future she would select the site with the aid of a
few other women. A committee on luncheon planning was
formed; the advantage, of course, was lots of lovely
lunches out!

SUMMARY

The early networks concentrate on atmosphere, on getting acquainted, and on learning about the professional lives of the members before organizational structure is formalized. The slow working out of NETWORK relationships is crucial to the eventual value of the organization: it is better to have a viable group that has taken time to cohere than a dynamic, go-getter bunch which will disintegrate because of lack of common bonds or personality clashes. Because networks are so new an idea for women, because the relationships must be set up so consciously, and because the feeling-out process is so hesitant, the critical ingredient is time. Getting to know each other, hearing about each other in a fairly structured way, and finding out that each woman is *one of us* are the major tasks of a successful NETWORK. After that, organization is easy: natural treasurers, like a gift of the gods, just emerge. Committees seem to form by mutual consent. Even recorders for the minutes appear—a phenomenon I have not noticed in organizations where women are relegated to secretary of this or that. The mutual harmony and great goodwill that develop among like-minded women in the course of time shows a spirit of cooperation that enables formal organization to emerge smoothly, credibly, and functionally quite perfect. Perhaps because the birth of a NETWORK is as fraught with both danger and promise as the birth of a child, the perfect birth seems a miracle of nature's efficiency.

Publishing a Directory

CHAPTER SEVEN

The first major accomplishment of the New Jersey NETWORK as well as of many other regional groups was the significant compilation, production, and distribution of an official directory. My NETWORK produced our "Golden Girl," so nicknamed because of the black print on gold paper, as our first official and formal act. It was as if we felt compelled to write ourselves into existence, a healthy process, and become visible to each other in print. A directory is also a subtle means of producing exclusivity, since no networks, including New Jersey, have plans for broad distribution of the directory. The basic purpose of the directory is to introduce members to each other, letting each one know the other's background, interests, and capabilities. Like birds parading their plumage, women networkers are parading intellectual, professional, and career colors. Without visible signs of achievement there must be some reference point for women successful in their own right who wish to communicate on a new basis. The urge to acquire visibility and legitimacy in print appears in networks formed both by regional groups and professional women's groups. Within an individual corporation, of course, there is no real need for a directory to provide this kind of visibility or ease of access; existing written material provides names, addresses, job titles, telephone numbers, and office locations. But for women loosely allied in their own professional groups, or pulled together on a geographical basis, the directory is a necessity. The ability to turn a good idea into a practical reality gave my NETWORK its major first-year boost. Our story is so similar to that of other networks throughout the country that the history of publishing a NETWORK directory is largely a record of the New Jersey group's experiences.

PUBLISH OR PERISH

NETWORK members seem to decide within the first six to nine months of meetings that a directory is necessary. Why? Two cover letters sent out along with questionnaires provide some answers. In a letter sent to New Jersey NETWORK members, I summarized the group feeling by stating: "It would be very valuable to produce a directory of NETWORK members, as a resource guide for each other. In our dual function of creating an internal NETWORK for peer support, and becoming a resource center for speakers, we ought to have the information we need at our fingertips." The New York Women's Bar Association, forming a NETWORK within a professional group of attorneys, stated its motives in quite similar form, also in a letter circulating with a questionnaire: "We discussed the need to have a more concrete reference of each others' interests as well as affiliations . . . . This NETWORK will become what we all make it and so we need to identify what each of us wants to get out of it."

There are big dreams in both of these purposes: a sense of making a NETWORK into something larger than itself. The regional group aspires to an outreach system into the community, the professional one into a job-sharing information clearing house. The big dreams, I think, will come true: networking is at the beginning of a groundswell of a new, important, and historic movement for the future of women. But the dreams begin with the immediate need for sharing information in an organized, accessible fashion: publication of a directory. The motivating forces are rather complicated and show some ambivalence. While networks want to reach out eventually, and while they have ambitious goals for the future, there is the opening impetus to hold on to this directory, to share information only with each other. The ambivalence centers around desire for, yet fears of exclusiveness as a criteria for membership: the old sorority syndrome.

There is the germ of exclusivity in the reluctance to share the directory with nonmembers, but an unwillingness to state the concept in so many words. We have circled the matter of selectivity, but no one has been willing, especially in writing, to say, "Look, we have to include some women, and exclude others. There are those who are simply not one of us." This refusal to say outright that networks operate on a selective basis could very well be an offshoot of a lingering distaste for the remembered sorority system of old: the very word sorority conjures up, to anyone over thirty-five and a product of the 1950s, pink angora sweaters, pearls, early marriages, and the success equals husband equation. In my own Ivy League background there were numbers of girls wandering around in our senior year, 1959, wearing raincoats in the summer over their sorority sweaters. The raincoats sometimes hid pregnancy in those preliberated, pre–sexual revolution days, and such dark secrets were kept by pact among the sisters. The concepts of *sisterhood* and *sorority* are extremely negative for NETWORK members, conjuring up memories of the fluffy, feminine mystique-laden, unprofessional fifties. There is no concept analogous to *fraternity*, *fraternalism*, and *fraternal*, good, strong, positive words denoting friendship, buddyhood, paldom.

A NETWORK cannot be a fraternity if it is to be a women's group. The English language does not permit that. Yet it cannot be a sorority if it is to be a serious organization of professional career women. Our mindsets do not permit that. Androgyny, a new option, is not only a concept unfamiliar to most women in the United States, but also a term which implies images of green-haired sexually indeterminate punk rock stars. At present, no sex-neutral terms define networks; the spirit is fraternal, but the mood is worlds away from anything smacking of the old sorority system. The ambivalence in the inability even to find a proper adjective is wrenching. How can we reach each other if we do not have the vocabulary with which to do it? We have no molds to fit into, no clear goals to aspire to, no ways of achieving palship that can bypass the sexual competitiveness of the 1950s. How do women get together in ways that provide professional input, advancement, and sharing, yet permit personal likes and dislikes and feelings of belonging as well? How, in other words, can women in networks elude the inapplicable fraternity connotations and the negative sorority connotations, and still come together to form a cohesive, helpful, sharing group?

The answer must be, as the NETWORK answers have been, to create totally new forms of grouping. An amazing phenomenon has been the spontaneous generation of networks all over the United States, and the startling similarities in all of this activity. And not least among these similarities is the relatively early NETWORK decision to publish a directory for use by the members. The desire to appear in print seems to be a basic urge in NETWORK activity, one which reflects a deeper need than ease of access to each other. Directories include more information than names, addresses, telephone numbers, and business affiliations.

The urge to publish is a response to an ambivalent and stress-laden situation. Women in networks refuse to judge each other on the basis of the obvious: clothing, speech, hairstyles, husbands, lifestyles. Yet they cannot ask each other directly, "Who are you? Where did you go to school? What do you do? What is your job title? I must know these things before I decide if you are one of us, and if I want to get to know you better." Networkers' spontaneous decisions to appear in print results from their desire to find out where each member is coming from, and if it is the same place for all.

I remember when I first read the copy for our own directory, I glowed with pride at every academic and career achievement of our members: the finer the background, the more outstanding the current position, the happier I was. And yet, even with my own heavily degreed credentials, in a prestigious but low-paying academic job, I always had the nagging feeling, "What am I doing here? How did I get into a group as impressive as this one?" I have since discovered that almost every other woman in my NETWORK has had the same feelings; we were all initially impressed by each other, and each felt that *she* was the outsider in a group of overachievers. Women in other networks keep mentioning the same reactions: they are impressed with the qualifications of other members and diffident about their own success. One woman in another suburban NETWORK said, "Until I saw the facts in print, I had no idea we were such a distinguished group. Then it took me three months to stop quaking because I felt sure I didn't belong. I felt like an imposter. Finally I had enough courage to say that since we were so special, we ought to think about closing rank and refusing admission to just anyone." This woman holds a high political appointive office: assistant to the governor of her state for a large suburban county. Yet she too alternated between feelings of self-deprecation and then assertions of legitimate elitism. Women have a difficult time accepting their career success on its own terms, and then taking their own achievements a step further in delineating their right to associate with like-minded networkers.

WHAT YOU SEE IS WHAT YOU GET

Thus the NETWORK impetus to publish a directory is complex and trails clouds of ambivalence; it is a way of establishing legitimacy, creating visibility, and parading professional plumage without actually stating exclusionary criteria in so many words. The directory is a professional calling card assuring us that our fellow NETWORK members are, indeed, one of us. We each can hold our own in this very select crowd. In a grouping where the forms of friendship are being created at the same time as the friendships are being formed, a means of visibility is essential. I do not think that directories will always be part of networks, but for the present, women who take themselves and their professional lives seriously have to establish this commitment on the printed page. The issuing of a *curriculum vita* is a bold step for those not engaged in a job hunt: it is a showing of colors to other women who might, by the way, find those colors unacceptably dim. But it is necessary as a formal, clear means of sharing information that women have no other shorthand means of sharing.

Because we have been so accustomed to judging each other on externals like clothing, manners, and ac-

cents, a clubby conversation like the following is still unlikely to occur between two women:

> X: "Hello, I'm X. Nice to meet you."
>
> Y: "Hello, I'm Y. Nice to meet you too. What do you do?
>
> X: "I'm in investment banking. And you?"
>
> Y: "Commodities. Banking, hm? Say, whose shop are
> you with?"
>
> X: "I'm a partner in 123, Limited; we keep a kind of low
> profile these days."
>
> Y: "I'll say! I'm with 789, Inc. myself; we're rather
> high-powered. I think one of our accounts is with
> your banker Z, isn't it?"
>
> X: "Sure! Z went to school with my partner W. In fact, I
> know Z myself from around town. We commute
> together some mornings."

Could X, Y, Z be women? EEO people would say, "Sure."
Are they women? Absolutely not! Never mind the minus-
cule numbers of women in investment banking and commodities houses. How many of them have become corporate partners? How many have gone to the same school?
How many live in the "right" towns and commute together? Even if the above were not the case, how many
women would hold a conversation like the above? Any
group where women have traditionally met in the past,
whether a luncheon club, alumni group, or even a professional association, has not been conducive to palship,
shop talk, or acquaintance-making. Women have traditionally gotten together, even professional career women,
and avoided helpful business discussions. There is a fear
of *public* discussion of business by women that has been a
powerful lever for keeping them down. Women have been
so reluctant to share shop talk in public that free exchange
of information has been almost nonexistent.

These conclusions are based on my own study of
business commuters' conversations. I find eavesdropping
on both the Manhattan subway and the more elite express

bus the perfect way to study career women's conversations. I also eavesdrop at random on men, who usually discuss business-related topics: the stock market, their functions within or related to it, current events pertaining to business, sports, and the weather. Interestingly enough, at the end of the day men are more inclined to discuss business; in the mornings, they talk about news and sports. My observations of the women are very different. Even the obvious Wall Street executive types, identifiable by expensive wool suits, silk blouses, closed pumps, and leather attache cases, are either sitting alone or discussing totally non–business-related topics, though steering clear of conventional girl talk. Women executives are unwilling to discuss business, money, or work-related activities in public. The clerical, sales, and nonmanagerial women, recognizable by dress, makeup, and hairstyle do discuss their jobs, their bosses, and their office relationships at great length. But the executive women either remain alone or speak together in pained and awkward generalities about nothing at all. They refuse to talk woman talk, are afraid to exchange business talk, and as a result their topics of conversation are severely limited. It is a long ride from Wall Street to Eighty-Sixth Street, and I have heard some desperately drawn-out conversations about the weather. I asked a friend, one of the NETWORK founders, about this avoidance of significant business talk in public: "In public, I am always super-careful never to mention what I do. You never know what sort of odd reaction people might have. I'm certainly not going to announce the fact that I'm a corporate auditor, a Columbia Business School alumna. After all, someone might be listening. And somebody might laugh, or ask me a question, or try to strike up a conversation. I'd rather discuss the weather, or read my newspaper."

Is this paranoia, or a healthy response to an insane city? I think neither. I think women refuse to state publicly their business credentials for fear of ridicule, hostility, and above all, *intrusion*. The opening-up, the sharing, does not at all come naturally for women in the sphere of professionalism. The whole process of career strutting is very new and done in very conscious, structured ways. Women who want to flaunt their professional feathers have to develop totally new ways of doing this; NETWORK formation is one way of woman to woman opening-up on a professional basis. The sexual sell implicit in sorority competition and cooperation can only be slowly, deliberately, and self-consciously replaced by achievement sell in new networks.

LET'S PLAY?

In many respects, the act of forming networks by women is a half-bold, half-hesitant publicizing of achievement, undercut by fears of rejection. It is akin to the child's hesitant question, on the verge of the sandbox, "Let's play?" The nonquestion question is typical of the tentativeness characteristic of female speech. Women talk either as if they expect to be ignored, or as if they expect approval only as questioners. It is the rare woman who can assert even her legitimate credentials in speech: "I am a surgeon. I went to New Jersey College of Medicine, and did my undergraduate at Vassar. After a residency at Mount Sinai, in New York, I began practice in Bergen County. I am now affiliated with Ridgewood Hospital and teach at Columbia Presbyterian Medical Center." A normal enough set of professional credentials for a doctor. Yet I cannot imagine, and have never heard, so dispassionate a recitation of background by a woman in ordinary speech. Many a woman can barely recite who she is without a nervous giggle, an attempt to downplay her qualifications, or both. For so many centuries, the woman's answer to the question, "Who am I?" has been, "John's wife and Tim and Máry's mother," that the new answers, "I am a brain surgeon," or "I am a nuclear physicist," do not come out easily. I can recall a colleague who always answered questions about her background with, "I got my doctorate from X University when X was worth going to and my subject worth some study." She is a historian with a doctorate from a major urban university, one of the top ten doctorate degree–granting universities in the United States; her degree in medieval history is of no small weight. But the very act of conveying nontraditional, non-role stereotyped answers to the question "Who am I?" puts even the most dedicated career woman on the defensive. For that reason alone, the publication of a NETWORK directory is beneficial as a means of shorthand introductions of one member to another. Since women are so diffident about proclaiming their own professional identities in public, a printed reference guide is an aid to comfortable sharing.

QUESTIONS, QUESTIONS

Do not let the joys of sharing information in print mislead you into thinking that the directory project is an easy one! The publishing part is relatively straightforward, since there will be a committee for that purpose, and within that committee, one person will probably take charge. Like all dictatorships, this one will work out efficiently. It is the questionnaire process preceding publication that is long-term and tedious. The questionnaires are easy enough to make up. Most of the information needed is routine: name; home address; home telephone number; business affiliation; business address; business telephone number. Both home and office addresses and telephone numbers are desirable, since a NETWORK is not limited to the contacts made during the work day; in fact, the work day may vary from profession to profession.

After these questions, there are also similarities in kinds of information needed. The questionnaire asks for "job functions," or "areas of expertise." In other words, What do you do? How do you do it? These require answers of more than one word. Simply writing, "attorney," or "advertising executive," is not sufficient, as the three lines allocated in the sample questionnaires indicate.

My regional NETWORK also requested names of other organizations to which the member belonged, for purposes of avoiding overlap with other groups; we were trying to see what other groups existed in New Jersey or even nationally that might be doing what NETWORK was planning to do.

Educational background was requested to provide some input on how women got to their present positions. We then asked what job-related and non–job-related subjects the respondent would be willing to speak on, for purposes of setting up a speaker's bureau. The Women's Bar Association questionnaire asked about format and content of the meetings, and also asked, "What subjects would you be willing to discuss and share with the group?"

The similarity in purpose of the questionnaires is clear: the questions are designed to elicit input from the members for each other's use. The thrust is, at least initially, exploratory. For a group planning to share information within the membership, each person must know the other's bailiwick. Although the regional New Jersey NETWORK does plan to set up a speaker's bureau, and as such has to know what its members feel qualified to speak on, and although the Bar Association plans to set up a career information exchange, and so has to know what everyone does and where she does it, the initial use of this information is for NETWORK membership sharing. Learning about each other, in a directory to be circulated to members only, is the unstated motive for questions that veer off from the strictly professional into the personal. What you do is not precisely the same question as what you would be willing to share with the group. The first deals with public matters that presumably the career woman would be willing to list, while the second deals with semipersonal, semicareer topics, such as balancing the commitments necessary to a husband, children, home, and career, which a woman might or might not want to bring out in front of a group.

NO ONE RAISED HER HAND

The major point about the NETWORK questionnaire is the time to be allocated for distributing it, receiving answers, and collating them into a published directory. At one point I felt certain that we would equal Thomas Carlyle's seventeen-year labor in producing his *History of the French Revolution*. The time for making up and distributing a questionnaire is approximately two days: one person makes it up and duplicates it; it is then mailed with a cover letter to the NETWORK members. So much for the mechanics of the questionnaire. It is a nice touch to add a stamped, self-addressed envelope for the convenience of respondents, since that saves the NETWORK member's time: she can fill in her answers and drop the completed form into the mail.

Unfortunately, only the mechanics are simple. What really happens is the proverbial teacher's nightmare: The teacher is in front of a classroom, and the university observation team determining tenure is in back. She asks a brilliant but not overly difficult question. The entire class sits there, blank, dull, and uncomprehending, as if no one had ever heard of the subject matter being discussed.

What does a NETWORK do when members do not respond to the questionnaire? In the New Jersey NETWORK, the members at a June meeting decided to publish a directory. By July, I had made up a questionnaire and sent it out to all the members. By November, I had received exactly three responses! Other networks have reported the same phenomenon: the idea of a directory is met with great enthusiasm, but no one sends back the completed questionnaire. Some networks have left blank questionnaires at the seats of each luncheon guest; after lunch, there were as many blank forms on the floor!

Why such a poor response? I do not know. Some members have handed me a resume, saying, "Just take the information you need from this." When I asked why *they* couldn't do that, I received these answers: "I have no time to fill out forms," "I really don't like questionnaires," and "I don't know what to put down after the basics."

It took six months to complete our directory. The questionnaire composition and distribution took place in July; the printing and mailing of the completed directory was done over two weeks in late December. The other five months were spent in frantic efforts to pull the information out of our members. We sent out two mailed notices, one requesting completion, one almost demanding it; in return we got checks for dues. Women networkers were apparently more eager to send money than information. Rather than abandon the directory project altogether, I decided to find the reason for this resistance and then figure out a way of overcoming it.

I came to some tentative conclusions about women's lack of confidence in self-assertion, even of readily obtainable information. It is again the difficulty of declaring one's identity, of saying who one is, in nontraditional areas. Once the automatic definition of wife and mother is removed and "occupation: housewife" no longer applies, women have a lot of difficulty in declaring themselves as career persons. They resist explaining their careers; they fear looking either insignificant or exaggeratedly important. I have heard the sentence, "What I do can't be explained easily," countless times; I realized that it is a peculiarly female thing to say. Men never say that; even men involved in jobs that aren't easily explained are happy to explain in great and often boring detail exactly what they do. Yet women have trouble summoning up their courage to explain their careers for fear of being judged petty, boring, abrasive, self-important, and a host of conflicting things. In the same moment, a woman will refuse to explain her work on the grounds that it is too hard to explain and too dull; yet she is also afraid that she will sound pompous or exaggeratedly egotistic. Women have not figured out that we are all selling; inventing a better mousetrap is of no use if no one knows about it. The self-effacement of even the most success-oriented woman is amazing, and emerges in an unwillingness, perhaps never dealt with squarely even in her own head, to declare what she does, what she is interested in, what she can share, and what she wants to know from others in her NETWORK. Hence, the uncompleted NETWORK questionnaires can torpedo the directory project almost from its inception.

TALKING IT OUT

Trying to understand this diffidence, and getting the completed questionnaires necessary to publish a directory, represented two very different tasks for me. My thoughts on the philosophy of networking followed the actual process of forming the New Jersey group and getting the directory together; but when faced with three completed forms, I had to figure out a way to tackle the practical problem, and let the philosophical underpinnings follow. I hit on a solution, which I cannot recommend wholeheartedly since it took an enormous amount of time and effort, but which I am proposing for desperate women who have run up against the dead end of a desired NETWORK directory, but no material for it. I realized that women who might be reluctant to write down their background, or reveal anything about themselves to a woman they did not know, would probably not refuse to cooperate in a personal survey. In other words, NETWORK members might respond to a personal phone call asking for information to complete the questionnaire. At least it was worth a try. When the directory committee met in November, we decided that two of us should take the membership list, about fifty in all, and simply telephone each woman. A committee member dropped a clue as to why we were having so much trouble eliciting responses: "You know, I just gave a speech at Wharton Business School, and I hated the formalities. I dislike speaking in public, and try to avoid it; I particularly hate being introduced to people as Mrs. *X*, financial analyst, *ABC* Corporation. The introductions make me feel dead; they sound like obituaries!" I realized that the questionnaire had not been sufficiently sensitive to other women's communication difficulties; as an extroverted academic, I regarded both writing and speaking in front of groups as the very best parts of my job. I had never considered the hesitancy most people have about speaking in public or autobiographically describing themselves. To get the directory published, then, we would have to consider NETWORK members' reluctance to parade their qualifications in print.

So, two NETWORK directory committee members involved in collecting information decided on the telephone route. We each had twenty-five names, and we gave ourselves a January 1 deadline for publication. We planned to use November to get the elusive questions answered, and then December for the mechanics of publication. Our third committee member was in charge of the actual publication: she is an advertising manager and a former copywriter, in command of both the writing and graphics end of production. The two telephone interviewers immediately began their project. I am happy to report that we had instant and gratifying results from all those women who were interested in remaining NETWORK members. An unexpected advantage of the direct call was pruning the list to weed out women no longer interested, as well as a compilation of additional names to consider. But the main purpose, filling in the content part of the questionnaire, worked out very well in a one-to-one phone call. The interviewees were quite receptive and willing to tell us what to put down in the blanks.

I did find that several areas of lack of confidence emerged. Many of the older women did not have the educational background currently required for their present position in a largely male world, possessed only an American Institute of Banking certificate. This situation is grees. A bank manager, one of the few women in her position in a largely male world, possessed only an American Institute of Banking Certificate. This situation is not unusual in banking, where women at the top today had to rise through the teller or clerical ranks, with little opportunity for education. The woman banker was quite hesitant about revealing what she perceived to be her lack of proper educational credentials: younger women in banking today, beginning at entry-level managerial slots, generally have a Master's degree in Business. The advantage of a direct call is that on the telephone it is both easy and true to say, "Your lack of an M.B.A. hardly matters: look where your A.I.B. certificate has taken you!" And so, the questionnaires were filled out with considerable ease by the two phone interviewers.

The questions about subjects the interviewee would be willing to speak on, for the eventual NETWORK speaker's bureau, raised more problems than any other. Many women did not want to speak out in public on *anything*. I have come to the conclusion that perhaps networking can do a great deal of good in its power to bring each member out, and, in effect, persuade her to give a public speech before a friendly, supportive audience. Given the nearly universal fears of speaking in public, the NETWORK practice in speech-making would be a direct benefit to career women who, if not actively held back by their reluctance to speak in public, certainly are not advanced by it. I did manage to convince the women I spoke to that public speaking was in no way mandatory. The NETWORK member need not address our group if she did not choose to, and she certainly would not be tapped as an outside speaker if she were disinclined to accept that role. Most of our NETWORK members eventually decided that they would speak on carefully delimited topics; only a few answered, "Do not wish to be a speaker."

Every other day I checked with the other NETWORK interviewer. I do not mean to give the impression that we spent all of our time on this, but I should warn prospective telephone callers to take on this work during their slow season! Huge amounts of time were spent simply connecting up with all of the women on our lists, in addition to filling out the forms. At a certain point, after about two weeks and at least fifty to seventy-five phone calls each, we arbitrarily decided to call a halt. Anyone who had not sent in a completed questionnaire by December 1, and had not responded to our phone messages, would not be in the directory. We decided, pretty much by fiat, that the directory would be updated annually, so that the frantic postdeadline wails, inevitable and predictable—"Why was I left out?"—could be answered by saying, "There's always next year's edition." As a matter of fact, most of our results took place within the first few days of calls; there seems to be a law of diminishing returns operating here as in other areas of business!

When we had collected twenty-five questionnaires from dues-paying members, we decided that we had enough material for our first NETWORK directory. We had originally planned to publish it in the form of a bound, paper-covered brochure, but decided not to do anything that permanent until the first update. We knew that after distribution of the first directory, those members not in it would clamor to be included. After the publicity that we expected to generate in the form of newspaper articles, we would also have to make serious decisions about membership that made a permanent directory at this stage an unjustifiable expense. Although we all liked the idea of something in book form—its permanence, stability, and solid respectability—we knew that the NETWORK was in its infancy, and major changes would take place within the next year. So although we had our hearts set on a production of *The New Jersey NETWORK Directory* as an enduring reference text, we settled for a much less permanent production: a photo offset, printed list of the charter members, encased in a cellophane binder.

THE FOUNDING MOTHERS

Those of us who were going to appear in the first directory dubbed ourselves the *founding mothers*; we considered ourselves the originators of a new kind of organization as surely as the founding fathers sired a new kind of state. The directory lists us as *charter members* because we took a more formal view of ourselves in print;

privately, we still refer to our nucleus as the founding mothers. We came to the decision to call the first publication, *Directory of Charter Members*, because of the amount of work and dedication put into the founding of the organization by the original two dozen women. We were pleased that this definition set us up as even more of an elite, an inner circle within a potentially larger power circle; we had gotten to the point of feeling that we deserved this recognition. Since a later series of decisions put the charter members in charge of the membership committee, we were in a position to create the kind of NETWORK group we felt would be most beneficial to all.

The founding mothers in charge of publication of the directory were involved in final decisions about type style, stock color, layout, and the dedicatory statement on the front cover. We decided to leave style and layout to the advertising executive in our midst. The front cover is reprinted here to show the final effect she achieved. The format of the pages is columnar: there are two columns, with the names listed in alphabetical order. There is no space between the listings for additional names, since we realized that any kind of planning for future membership would be impossible unless we went to looseleaf form, with one entry per page. If we did that, we would have extra problems in binding, as well as higher paper and postage bills. So we opted for a form that looks permanent enough, since names cannot be added, but which will have to be completely revised and reset within the year. A few of the founding mothers muttered about the "permanence of impermanence" but went along with our decision.

We did engage in extensive discussion about colors: black print on white stock was deemed ordinary, and neither pink nor blue stock was a serious contender. Someone did suggest pink as parody, but most of us insisted that the point would be missed by virtually everyone. *I* missed the point of a new *Women's Studies Journal* whose cover was printed in heliotrope ink on lavender paper. In fact, I wrote to the editor and suggested that this color combination was singularly unfortunate in connotation; she wrote back and said that I did not understand the humor, for the colors were an ironic comment on Victorian lavender and old lace. I am not at all sure that even in today's advanced climate serious journals can afford to use color humorously and then be taken quite seriously. As a result of this preconception, or perhaps misconception, I automatically veto pink or blue for any NETWORK communique. Using colors which are traditionally gender-tied is, I think, foolish. After much debate and some laughter, the founding mothers dared to choose *gold*. The black print on goldenrod stock produced a very professional, exciting looking directory.

There was one last problem: writing the cover blurb, the dedicatory statement. I received a frantic letter in early December from the advertising executive, who said that she was having more problems with the prose than if she were writing the Preamble to the Constitution. We wanted to be both brief and hard-hitting, and could not seem to elucidate our goals in ad copy style. We decided to forget extreme brevity and snappy slogans, and to work with complete sentences and a detailed goal statement. That seemed to work out well: distillation of NETWORK ideals into twenty-five words or less proved impossible, so we put an eight-line statement on the front cover. Once that decision was made, we were ready to go to print.

At that point the advertising executive took over. She sent the material to her graphics shop, personally supervised the layout and production, picked up the finished copies, and delivered them to our NETWORK headquarters. They were mailed out to members the first week in January, only a few days past our deadline! The reactions were unanimously favorable: every member, even those most reluctant to provide information, was impressed by the professional production of the directory as well as by the quality of women represented. We crowed for quite a while, proud of each other and ourselves, and our ability to produce a first of this kind. This first directory of NETWORK charter members remains a source of pride for all of us, as well as a useful document: we use the directory frequently for telephone numbers, women to provide information in specific areas of expertise, and women to provide contacts for other women.

Not a week goes by when some NETWORK member is not connected up with another; in many cases, the contacts are made almost daily. The lawyer and the banker lunch together regularly; the stockbroker and the accountant have developed a working relationship. The dentist gives her law business to the all-woman law partnership, and the realtor has been the broker in several home sales for clients referred to her by all of the above. I have called on many women in the NETWORK for a television series I did for CableVision. I wanted to interview women experts who could help newly single widows and divorcees in suburbia, so I thumbed through the directory to see who was available and willing to go before the TV cameras. Because so many of the NETWORK members were guests on the show, the group informally nicknamed the TV series, "NETWORK Goes NETWORK." The interview schedule looked like a roster of the founding mothers.

Our directory has turned out to be a useful means of keeping information about each other at our fingertips. In many ways other than its color, it has become New Jersey network's "Golden Girl," a new kind of achievement status symbol. Production of a directory is an excellent first formal step for any NETWORK to take, since it requires the cooperation of all, the leadership of a few, and the establishment of an *esprit de corps* within the group.

The parading of career goals and achievements by one woman to another, the publicizing of professional commitment as a lifestyle, represents an enormous source of pride to each member. This directory is a visible symbol of achievement both in itself—we produced a book of our own—and in its contents—we are quite an impressive group of women. Perhaps before we saw ourselves collectively in print, we felt diffident, self-conscious, and hesitant about flaunting our colors. Now that we have each other as reference points and can point to the successes we have each achieved in our own spheres, we have all grown in confidence. The company one keeps in many ways determines one's outlook; by writing ourselves up as members of a successful, elite, career-oriented group, we have come to recognize our own legitimate aspirations and destinies. The NETWORK directory was a long time in the making, but it is a document of great power. We look at ourselves anew, with pride and confidence not only in our own professional capabilities, but also in our ability to NETWORK with other women who are experts in other spheres. We've created a new "Golden Girl," but unlike the one which merely glittered, our achievement is solid, twenty-four karat, and enduring. And we have a directory to prove it!

New Jersey
NETWORK

DIRECTORY OF CHARTER MEMBERS

New Jersey NETWORK is a group of women from both the business and professional fields, dedicated to the dual goals of peer support and outreach. Peer support enables us to make contact with each other and consolidate our individual resources - information, experience, and influence - so that each can help each. Outreach permits us to help the achievement-oriented woman by educating her to advance career commitment as a life goal. Our NETWORK thus represents both a mutual support system and an educational service for the dedicated, ambitious, forceful executive women of today and tomorrow.

NEW JERSEY
NETWORK QUESTIONNAIRE

Name _____

Home Address _____ Phone _____

_____

_____

Business Affiliation _____

Title of Position _____

Business Address _____ Phone _____

_____

_____

Job Functions/Professional Specialty _____

_____

_____

Professional Organizations (include positions held, if any)

_____

_____

_____

_____

Civic/Cultural Organizations _____

_____

_____

_____

_____

Educational Background _____

_____

_____

On what job-related subjects would you be prepared to speak?

(Attach a short summary if possible) _____

_____

On what non-job related subjects would you be prepared to speak?

_____

_____

NEW YORK WOMEN'S BAR ASSOCIATION INFORMATION FOR NETWORK DIRECTORY

Name _____

Position _____

Firm/Co. _____

Address _____

Office phone: _____ Home phone: _____

Areas of expertise _____

_____

_____

Areas of interest _____

_____

_____

New York Woman's Bar Association Questionnaire for Network List (Distributed June 27, 1979).

Suggestions for
Meeting Format/Content

Format: How would you like to see our meetings structured?

_____

Content: What subjects would you like to hear discussed? __

_____

_____

What subjects would you be willing to discuss/share with the
group? _____

_____

What times are best for us to meet? _____

Do you know of any place we could meet regularly? _____

Bring completed questionnaire to next luncheon.

Founding a Lunch Club

CHAPTER EIGHT

THE THREE R'S

The motivation for an official lunch club sorts itself out as a desire for a new set of three r's: relaxation, recognition, and respectability. The need for relaxation at lunch time is closely allied with a place to relax: temporary quarters breed anxiety simply because they are temporary. When the New Jersey NETWORK was meeting in the conference room of the lawyers who had been instrumental in founding the group, we were comfortable enough. Yet we found ourselves increasingly impelled to set up a more formalized, more structured official club atmosphere. Other networks which have also begun with ad hoc, spontaneous arrangements for lunch have been, in the course of time, equally inspired to leave temporary quarters no matter how delightful. The moving spirit is complex, but it is undeniable that members relax when they have a regular meeting place. People like the security of knowing that they have a particular place that is their own. Security, comfort, and the sigh of relief that is associated with "coming home" are all achieved in a club atmosphere that is specifically a NETWORK lunch spot.

There is also a desire for the second r: recognition. When a NETWORK has become a cohesive entity, it wants to make itself publicly known as such. In the case of the New Jersey NETWORK, this motive surfaced just after we published and distributed our directory. Since we had declared ourselves to be a group of serious, dedicated career professionals, we were now convinced of our own visibility, significance, and importance, and were confident enough to tackle the project of establishing a lunch club. First we declared ourselves a NETWORK in print; then we went on to carve out a physical space for ourselves. Even in an intracorporate NETWORK, the move to found a lunch club involves not necessarily a physical removal from the board room, but a removal of the temporariness of senior management's lending that room for just one meeting. The corporate NETWORK aims at the recognition of its meetings as a regular event, by having the board room set aside on a monthly basis, at a specific time, for NETWORK members' use. The corporate NETWORK is saying, in effect, "Look at me! I exist! I have a right to a space that is mine and mine alone at certain times." This is the *Room of One's Own* manifesto, and every woman knows instinctively what Virginia Woolf expressed: people need their own money, time, and space in order to feel that they exist. The very act of requesting the corporation's most elegant room for a regular NETWORK group, as opposed to sporadic usage of it when the men are not there, is a demand for recognition. If the NETWORK has been functioning in a serious, professional way and makes its bid for recognition in an acceptable fashion, nine times out of ten the board room will be set aside for its use at the stated time. In one intracorporate NETWORK, the women felt great trepidation at asking for the board room every month for a luncheon; they were so fearful of rejection that they drew straws to see who would be the lucky woman who got to ask the executive vice president. The result was anticlimactic: the vice president said, with some puzzlement, "I thought you were using it the first Wednesday anyway, weren't you?" Luckily, the questioner realized that she was giving up a little too much independence, visibility, and recognition for her NETWORK and countered with, "Yes, but we wanted to switch to Tuesdays, and thought we'd clear it with you first." Recognition means never having to ask for your space every month!

In the case of a professional women's group, such as financial women, or women lawyers, the need for permanence and recognition also occurs, but the logistics are more difficult. The sporadic use of a conference room in one member's corporation or another member's government office becomes unsatisfactory after a certain amount of time. During the months when networkers are exploring goals, interests, careers, and lifestyles, temporary quarters work out well enough. But once the temporary aspects of the group fade, borrowed quarters, no matter how pleasant, lush, or convenient simply do not work. The urge to permanence manifests itself in a desire for either distinct space or regular use of borrowed space. In the case of professional women's groups, neither option is really open: No one corporation or government bureau has the obligation, moral or otherwise, to lend space with regularity to a group of women, most of whom are unconnected with the lender. And, surely a law firm or corporation is not going to turn over a conference room to a professional women's group for permanent use! While the intracorporate NETWORK has a clear claim to the board room, and a regional NETWORK can graciously accept the donation of a conference room of one of its members, it is much more difficult for a group of women organized into a professional group to settle into that kind of space. Professional women's groups tend to move from restaurant to department store to bank looking for a suitable slot; their wanderings gradually lose the sense of adventure and simply become an annoyance.

TEMPORARY QUARTERS

The degree of irritation felt at temporary quarters is worth looking into, since every NETWORK I have encountered has shown the need for the recognition a permanent lunch club implies. I have often asked myself why my own regional NETWORK felt dissatisfied with the conference room, why a corporate NETWORK feels annoyed by the need to make monthly requests to use the conference room, why a professional group's NETWORK moves from place to place, looking for a proper spot. There is a degree of irritation in the reaction to temporary quarters which seems out of proportion to the situation. In no case I have seen has a NETWORK been particularly uncomfortable in a conference or board room. Although the networks that choose public lunch spots with private rooms are taking a chance, some restaurants do have excellent private facilities. The problem is the risk and rejection factor. Each time and each place represents a new set of chances, and possible successes or failures. Even repeated requests for the board room or the conference room of a member's firm represent a possible "no," a potential rejection. This possibility seems to hit a basic level of insecurity that gradually makes the NETWORK members more and more uncomfortable.

In addition to the insecurity that causes a lack of ease, there is a whole complex of feelings that can be summed up under the third r of respectability that networks aim at. What networks want is recognition by the general public of their existence as professional career women's groups. This recognition involves a twofold change in attitude: divesting the group of women from sex-role stereotypes they feel, as well as from sexual responses they arouse in observing males. All publicly perceived sex-related connotations must be eliminated: woman the provider, woman the nurturer, woman the sex object all have to be ignored as stereotypes if women as networkers are to achieve respectable status as business persons helping other business persons. Unfortunately, the world has not yet caught up to the theory of non-stereotyped women. Women in groups are viewed—and view themselves—in stereotyped roles. They see themselves as nurturing, sexually attractive, providing types; the theory of the independent, self-reliant, professional career woman simply does not fit in with these self-images and world views. Establishing a new image involves defusing the old stereotypes of woman as the provider of food and sex. These images, and the need to defuse them, erupt with full force in the subject of founding a lunch club. The whole matter is fraught with tension because of the associations of women with food and sex that form the substructure of male and female minds alike. Founding a lunch club for a women's NETWORK is fraught with problems, not because founding a lunch club is terribly difficult: it isn't. The problems are all of the old hangups, the psychological cobwebs which surround and sometimes immobilize women in the areas of food and sex.

Lady Libbers

I finally saw the full importance of the lunch club and the three r's of relaxation, recognition, and respectability for networks in an incident in a restaurant in New York's chic summer resort, the Hamptons. This is the sophisticated New York City summer scene, the Upper East Side with sand. I was dining with a woman friend at a popular restaurant in Bridgehampton, on a midweek evening. Like many restaurants, this one had a long bar area which diners had to traverse to get to their tables. We were walking out of the restaurant, through the bar, when I spotted Betty Friedan sitting down at a table. Ms. Friedan is one of my all-time culture heroines, a woman whom I consider the most important theoretician of women's issues of the past decades, and I exclaimed enthusiastically, "There's Betty Friedan! I heard she bought a house out here, but never expected to see her in as public a place as this one—I've heard she is a very private person." The minute I mentioned the name—"Betty Friedan"—a well-dressed man at the bar turned to me and said, "You one of those lady libbers, huh?"

Why form a lunch club? So that women in networks can relax, bask in the recognition of their achievements, and feel the sense of respectability to which they are entitled *without* having to cope with all of the negative associations of "lady libbers." These associations, the thought patterns that connect Betty Friedan with bra-burning, castrating harpies, are not backwoods mindsets of ancient redneck males. The prevailing male mentality—still, in spite of growing numbers of women in careers—is patriarchal, role-dominated, connected with stereotyped men and women. Men today are probably more confused than women by the growing numbers of women who want not only to be in the work force, but to succeed there; nevertheless, the world is in a transitional stage, and by no means as advanced in the direction of equality as optimistic media news would have us believe.

Why should networks have their own lunch clubs? So that the women members can avoid tension, invisibility, and intrusion. "Lady libbers" is a putdown, and a form of psychological rape. Women should have a place to go to be free of such attacks, if only for two hours. To be able to say what we think as professional and career women, to admire our own heroines, and to protest against the more abrasive elements of male-dominated society without being called "lady libbers" are legitimate NETWORK goals.

A PLACE OF OUR OWN

In order to achieve those goals, which used to be called freedom of speech, women need a place of their own, a clubhouse. Networkers want a place to go for lunch where no one will call us "lady libbers," where we can relax, secure in our own lifestyles and free from intrusion. We need a place in which we can feel comfortable and in command. This is a natural extension of the desire to take a break at midday, to refresh the spirit as well as the body, in a relaxing, easy, pleasant atmosphere. This is also part of a barely articulated desire to be taken care of graciously, as is our due. Women in networks are so used to perceiving themselves as the sole providers of food, and of course food equals love, that it is quite a psychological jolt for us to realize that we have the right to want to be provided for during at least one meal of the day. As successful women we have a legitimate need for recognition in the form of good food, good service, and good atmosphere. We want to be served good food with a minimum of fuss and tension. It is women's decision to claim this right that causes so much ambivalence in the founding of a lunch club.

The universal desire for relaxation, recognition, and respectability in connection with food and comforts is the reason for the existence of men's clubs. The moving spirit behind men's clubs, traditionally, has been the desire of members to have a place of their own. A man's club has been his real castle; he could always count on the peace, comfort, decent food and often lodging a club provided, even when his home was in turmoil. Historically it has been the great escape valve, not only for lunch, but often for breakfast and dinner, as well as for companionship, a night's sleep, exercise, recreation, and perhaps sex. While I am not suggesting that networks try to duplicate the original British, and later American copies, of the traditional men's club, I am suggesting that the motives are similar. Women, like men, need a place of their own. And women in networks, representatives of what seems to be the start of a totally new order of things, are just beginning to carve out for themselves traditional rights that men have accepted for centuries. Men in clubs have made absolutely no bones about not only the creature comforts they demanded—everything from satisfying meat and potatoes menus to elaborate exercise facilities—but also about the people with whom they want to share these comforts. In one word, men's clubs have been *exclusionary*; members have been easily able to exclude anyone who did not fit into the category of *one of us*: blacks, Jews, Catholics, women, all or any of the above. This kind of thinking is very foreign to women, and is considered in a separate section on membership. At this point, it is necessary to mention that the very basis for clubs is an exclusionary set of criteria: some are in, some are not.

Women have been taught that this exclusionary behavior is not nice. If women in networks do not actually say the word, they are thinking it. Perhaps women who have achieved power in traditionally male enclaves—and all power enclaves are male ones, except for the home—have become savvy enough to know that you do not reach the top, or even the middle, through niceness. But in the peculiar mix of business and personal relationships that networks represent, the element of niceness is present, even if not articulated. It comes up, without being directly expressed, in the matter of lunch clubs. Why should women who have achieved success have to expose themselves to the humiliation of remarks about "lady libbers"? They do not! The essence of a club is that it is filled with people like you, people you like to be with, and people with whom you feel at home while dining. Women who have gained viable careers have earned the right to lunch with whom they want; they have also earned the right to exclude those they do not want, which is the story of membership.

The motivating spirit for a lunch club is the career woman's desire not only for a place of her own, but also for a publicly recognized place. This lunch club activity is a response to the desire to be recognized: the networks want recognition as groups of achieving women. And the desire for recognition takes the form of having, in effect, a known clubhouse where some women can enter and others cannot. Once the motives are sorted out, once the psychological ambivalences are examined, some concrete steps can be taken to gain access to such a place. Relaxation, recognition, respectability: women are entitled to these rewards just as men are. Just as men in clubs have earned their club membership, so women in networks have also earned their rights.

THE BUSINESS LUNCH

Once the three r's were brought out and discussed in the regional New Jersey NETWORK, our move out of the private law offices became not only clearer as a desired goal, but also inevitable. What seemed to be an enviable situation—a private dining room, in effect, within the confines of an all-woman law firm—was perceived as not at all suitable. Even though we could invite anyone we wished, eat whatever food we desired, run interference with no one at all, the setup was not suitable. Relaxation was not totally possible: the lawyers and their staff had to take care of ordering the food, setting the table, passing around the platters, and cleaning up. Once again, it was woman the provider, and, even more unfairly, always the same woman! Making sure that we had nourishing, varied meals became the task of our own members, and it was not only unfair, but also annoying. The corporate law partner summed up all our feelings when, in an uncharacteristic burst of temper, she said, "If anyone drops another oily piece of lettuce on our carpet, she can clean it up herself! This is a law office, not a restaurant!" Those of us who had so casually accepted the burden of providing lunch realized that she was on target: we had a perfect right to let others handle the food business, while we concerned ourselves with our *business* business!

So we grew impatient with the food logistics: How could we vary the menu without facilities for hot food? Should we use paper plates and silver utensils? Who would be responsible for cleaning up the mess? After our directory was finished, we also became concerned about the lack of recognition our totally private lunch club might be doomed to. We had no physical room for expanding the membership: the conference table was limited in size. But more important, who would *know* that New Jersey NETWORK had formed a lunch club if it was so private, so tucked away, that no opportunities for publicity existed? If we could not expand, we could not publicize. And if we could not publicize, we could not achieve recognition. One of our members has as her goal an additional announcement posted on the "Welcome to *X* Town" sign: Not only is there a "Rotary Lunch at 12 Noon" and a "Kiwanis Lunch at 1 P.M.," but also a "NETWORK Lunch at 12 Noon on Alternate Thursdays"! While this seems a little futuristic, our group felt that attention, respect, and public awareness of our existence were inextricably tied in with the founding of an outside lunch club.

Publication of the directory forced us to focus on the general, widespread, and specifically female problems that the business lunch poses. We had all thought that this time-honored ritual was difficult as an individual matter; once we began sharing input, sharing ideas about common career difficulties, we quickly realized that the business lunch was a horror for us all, in various ways. Undoubtedly that first view of our directory over the lunch table triggered the specific associations of a business lunch for many of us: We all had experienced salad dressing trailed over important documents, embarrassing moments at bill-paying time, and the unsuitable quality of semidarkness at noon for transacting business in a restaurant. But we had not realized that these difficulties were common ones. We had also not realized the need for a lunch club for NETWORK *guests*, not only members. All of us had occasion to take colleagues, associates, and clients out to lunch at one time or another, and none of us had really handled the problem of the business lunch with total ease. NETWORK decided to form a lunch club not only for access to each other, but also as a way of handling the business lunch for all of us.

Our regional, interdisciplinary NETWORK needed a lunch club as a place to take guests, since virtually all of us were responsible for some business entertaining. Naturally, our temporary quarters were not suitable for that purpose: even the lawyers did not use their own conference room for lunches! The need for business lunch places where career women can comfortably take prospective customers, clients, and business acquaintances has not even been measured accurately: most men, women, and even restuarateurs have not perceived the problem. A business lunch can form one of the most tense periods of the day for a woman, simply because the mechanics are so difficult. The existing difficulties should be considered by networks to see just why founding a lunch club is so very desirable. Most of the difficulties can be grouped under the heading, *respectability*. The business lunch is high on the woman executive's stress scale because the association of women and sex seems to dog those women who must entertain at lunch. In a word, any woman in a public place can be judged fair game for sexual innuendo: she may *not* actually receive a proposition, but the possibility always exists as an unpleasant intrusion. Alternatively, any woman in a ladies' lunch spot is judged somehow trivial, non–career committed, probably not even working. "Ladies" do not work, although they tend to congregate in a completely nonserious way, a way that filters through to the woman trying to conduct serious business at lunch. There is no option for women in networks except to found their own lunch clubs, with their own particular club spirit prevailing.

Lunch in a public restaurant is a direct threat to the careful nonsexuality of the business woman. The serious disadvantage of a public restaurant is, obviously, that it is public: the woman executive or professional runs the risk of unfriendly, unwarranted comments simply by her being there. If the woman is early, and decides to wait at the bar, she becomes a lone woman sitting on a bar stool. A woman physician, marketing manager of a Fortune 500 company, or professor does not wear her title like a label: at a bar, she is merely an available woman. There is very little that is more embarrassing than having to fend off a lunch time proposition, generally for a "quickie," while simultaneously greeting a business acquaintance. The tension involved in waiting for one's lunch companion to arrive can only be gauged by women who have experienced it. One San Francisco lawyer, a very attractive and chic cosmopolitan woman, told me that she always waited for clients at the maitre d's station, midway between the bar and the dining room at lunch time. She had learned *not* to wait at bars because of her own feelings about being "meat on the meat rack." She said, and I admired her frankness, "Being judged as a sex object completely destroys my appetite for business, let alone lunch. I need a clear head to conduct a business lunch, and try to avoid any distractions."

Sitting alone at a table is not much better: the woman executive is visibly alone, and no matter how confident she is, she is well aware that being alone signals being *unwanted* to other people. Even if the successful woman has crossed off opinions of other people long ago, the annoyance at having to play with a drink, do imaginative things to bread sticks, smoke a cigarette builds as the lone woman diner waits for her business acquaintance to show up. Again, the mood is not conducive to good business.

The last option—perpetual lateness—is no better: that is judged in many cases as inexcusable rudeness, or female giddiness. There is no satisfactory way of dealing with the problems of meeting clients or colleagues at a public luncheon spot. Even if the grand finale—settling the bill—has been smoothly arranged, the tension associated with waiting in a restaurant is often enough to throw a damper on the business lunch. It becomes increasingly clear why so many women executives and professionals have chosen to eat alone. If a NETWORK lunch club can make the business lunch a situation where the woman has at least the same chance for comfort as the business man does, it will be performing a great service.

While lunch in a public place often exposes the businesswoman to the concept of lunch as a four-letter word, lunch at the standard women's club is no more relaxing or respectable in the sense of avoiding a stereotype. A women's club, city or country, is a rather impossible place for business entertaining. No client wants to be surrounded by a gaggle of ladies discussing flabby thighs and fashions. Just as men's clubs are bastions of business men's man talk, money talk, power talk, so women's clubs are bastions of lady talk, snob talk, kiddie talk. The woman who wants to discuss the latest treatment for flabby thighs would feel no more comfortable in the Yale Club than the man who wants to discuss the latest way to *sell* this new treatment would feel in the local women's club. Neither men nor women in business or the professions feel particularly comfortable in women's clubs. Men, obviously, are very nervous in the presence of an all-woman lunch situation; it would be folly to bring a man with whom one has a business relationship into a women's club. Seriously committed career women are also put off by this atmosphere: there is tension there, an interwoman clash of lifestyle, that surfaces unpleasantly. Women achievers feel residual hostility at the large numbers of women still dedicated, it would seem, to lunch and the thinner thigh, the concept of creative leisure. I know that in the middle of my own day, when I feel that tight band of pressure around my forehead caused by conflicting and often irreconcilable demands of career, home, children, and deadlines, I react with strong hostility to women who make no more demanding decisions than what to cook for dinner and what to wear to a P.T.A. meeting in the same week. And I don't want to have to feel this tension at lunchtime! NETWORK women have enough stress in their single, double, triple, even quadruple roles without having to deal with ambiguities posed by a women's lunch club.

DO IT YOURSELF!

Public restaurants, then, as well as women's clubs are not very comfortable places to bring clients and colleagues for a business lunch. What then can career women do? How can women in networks achieve relaxation, respectability, recognition in their lunch endeavor? At the risk of being accused of reinventing the wheel, I can only say that the answer must be, "Found your own club." The regional New Jersey NETWORK faced the problem of reinventing the wheel and agreed that it had to be done. We knew that we had to found a lunch club both for our own meetings and for business entertaining. In spite of the plethora of eating places that exists, the NETWORK will not find what it wants unless it creates it. The qualities we sought were elegance, comfort, and privacy, criteria hardly revolutionary for clubs, by the way! Our problem, and that of most other networks in the United States, was that in suburban areas few such clubs existed. Does this sound hard to believe? Our NETWORK thought so. When we decided to found a lunch club, we assumed we would have no difficulty in finding a suitable existing club—either a country club, a men's club that needed money as well as a display of goodwill towards women, a college or university club—to which we could attach ourselves. Not so! The country clubs that were nearby were far too expensive to join, and not at all businesslike at lunch: most of the lunch guests were women or retirees. There were no men's clubs, such as New York's Racquet and Tennis or University Club, which might have chosen this opportunity to desegregate inspired by the carrot of more lunch covers. And, there were no nearby college or university clubs, again typical of suburban locales: this sort of club is associated primarily with cities. As far as the local women's club was concerned, one NETWORK member said, "If you remain seated for too long at lunch, the directress throws a tea cozy over you, attaches a price tag, and sells you at the Christmas craft festival." So much for attaching oneself to existing clubs.

The option of setting up a lunch club within an existing restaurant was about the only one left. For most networks, this will be the bottom line. A NETWORK can adopt the "do it yourself!" spirit only partially at this time, and will have to find a nearby restaurant within which to form a lunch club. Lacking an existing and suitable club-like facility to latch onto, a NETWORK lunch club must either find a restaurant to append itself to, or get into real estate (more about that futuristic, but very likely solution, later on). The critical question then becomes, within *which* restaurant can a NETWORK form a lunch club? The question is critical because even when faced with thousands of choices, the essential fact is that the spirit of the restaurant affects the NETWORK lunch club. Again, a psychological cobweb, a source of ambiguity, a need to cope with am-bivalence is foisted upon NETWORK members. The choice of restaurant depends in large part on atmosphere, on intangibles which the women careerists may not even fully articulate. Just as the Ladies' Temperance Society can not meet above the local saloon without losing all credibility, and just as that situation is terribly unfair, no NETWORK can afford to establish a lunch club in any milieu that does not actively provide relaxation, recognition, and respectability.

CONVENIENCE FOODS

Convenience sometimes turns out to be a luxury that networks cannot afford in their choice of lunch club sites. Almost every American suburb sports highway res-taurants, real restaurants as opposed to fast-food estab-lishments, that fairly shout "Convenience!" because of ease of access, adequate parking facilities, and realistic prices. One of our NETWORK members suggested just such a restaurant, with a private room, on a major highway intersection convenient to women traveling from all parts of the county. Unfortunately, this happily married woman was blissfully unaware of the restaurant's reputation as the most notorious singles' bar west of Manhattan! Although this bar scene took place primarily at night, and lunch patrons looked as if they were going about the business of business, the objections to such a spot were serious ones: the aura of swinging singles would drastically undercut the serious career orientation of a lunch club formed by business, professional, and academic women. No NETWORK can risk guilt by association; we can deplore it, but we cannot risk it. Any site selected must have untarnished respectability. Networks must present a nononsense business image to the world. As members of the first such women's lunch club in the county, New Jersey networkers could not afford to be associated with a singles' bar. The geographical convenience, which probably aided the successful singles' scene as well, would have to be foregone. So a NETWORK has to compromise: accessibility and reasonable pricing may have to give way, to avoid the travelling salesman connotations, snickers and smirks when the lunch club site is announced.

For very similar reasons, networks throughout the United States try to avoid restaurants in nearby hotel, motel, and shopping center complexes. In America, dining out is so homogenized that given the demographics for an area, one can accurately predict the kinds of feeding facilities that exist. Networks thus have very similar problems in almost any suburban and city areas, since their choices are governed by what already exists, and that is quite uniform wherever one goes. Because women in networks have to avoid any sexual overtones in a lunch club, hotels and motels are probably very unwise choices. It may be unfair, but it is the way of the world. Networks are not out to reform society, but to operate effectively within whatever structure exists. If women in networks want to be taken seriously as dedicated career persons, helping each other as well as younger and less experienced women, they have to bend over so far backwards to avoid sexual connotations that they must put up with geographical inconvenience, high prices, even a greater or lesser degree of isolation than desired simply to avoid *any* undesirable sexual associations. For that reason, hotel and motel sites—either restaurants or private rooms—should be avoided if possible, unless, as in some suburbs, there are no alternatives whatever. Shopping center restaurants, for the opposite reason—they are almost exclusively patronized by nonworking women during the day—should also be avoided. Both the singles' hangout and the ladies' lunch room are undesirable for the NETWORK lunch club image. This generally translates into the need to choose a spot that is more inconvenient as well as more expensive than either of the above.

URBAN BLIGHT

City networks, which have similar problems when it comes to assuring respectability, do have an option generally not available to suburban groups: the city club. Several groups of women in networks of professional women, corporate women, and even regional women within a large city have wrestled with the lunch club problem. They have considered private rooms in restaurants, private women's clubs, and private men's or college clubs. The first two have been vetoed for all of the reasons given so far. The option of forming a lunch club attached to a prestigious city club has been taken up in some instances. One NETWORK has formed a lunch club within the halls of a very prestigious university club in a medium-sized city. I attented a meeting of this NETWORK to find out what sort of attraction that club held, how a lunch club for women within a predominantly men's club worked, and what the general feeling about the atmosphere was. The attraction the club held, the reason the NETWORK wanted to meet and dine at this status-laden men's club, was, in one word, *prestige*. Instead of guilt by association, this was glory by association: the NETWORK movers felt that by their very admission into this club, even on a limited basis, they would inherit the mantle of power that the male members normally wore. The formation of a women's NETWORK lunch club within what had previously been an all-male club of the most supreme overachievers, the iviest of the Ivy Leaguers, was considered a great plum, a coup for the NETWORK women. The women in this city NETWORK, a regional one consisting of the one hundred most eminent women in that city, had been determined to form their lunch club under the aegis of the most powerful, most prestigious, most elite men's club they could find. The way they did it was quite simple: Two graduates of the recently turned coeducational university went to the club's board of directors and reminded them that the university had recently been under a lot of pressure to do more for women. This dictum had already mandated the admission of women members into the formerly all-male city club for alumni. Certainly, they said, and I am paraphrasing a fairly remarkable conversation here, the incorporation of a NETWORK lunch club into the current structure would gain a great many points for them.

The logistics would not be difficult, the persuasive networkers went on to say. A room could be set aside for the use of NETWORK, billing facilities could be developed for NETWORK members apart from those for regular club members, limited-basis membership for NETWORK women could be created, and the public announcement of a club-within-a-club could be made. The NETWORK proposal was made in time-honored business fashion: the bottom line was public pressure on this group of men to do more for women. Networkers offered them a solution to this problem involving a minimal expenditure of money to gain a maximal return of helpful publicity, as well as a bagful of good deeds to show to whatever Women in Government Commission happened by. The move was so outrageous, well-timed, well-planned, and well-executed, that it succeeded. In near-record time, the women's NETWORK had created a lunch club within what had been for close to two centuries the impregnable walls of the leading men's club on the eastern seaboard.

What exactly was accomplished by this city NETWORK? How does it feel to conduct business lunches in this atmosphere? How does it feel to to have NETWORK meetings within these walls? What is it like to be one woman among several hundred men? One woman with a male client in an all-male preserve? One woman with a female client? Fifty women holding a lunch meeting? When I was a guest at such a NETWORK meeting, I felt *strange*. I had that queasy, not quite belonging sense of displacement. I spoke to other women who felt the same way; the air was tense, frazzled, harried. These clubs have spirit, but the spirit seems all wrong for relaxation, comfort, ease where women are concerned. The women I spoke to felt like interlopers: conspicuous, combative, almost having to fight for their right to breathe the same air as the "real "members. While I fully understand the women's NETWORK feeling that it is their *right* to form a lunch club within a club where some of them are legitimate members by dint of having graduated from the university in question, the right to be there is not synonymous with comfort. One member who never went to NETWORK lunches any more, summed up her feelings this way: "I don't want to defend my identity every three steps: the doorman looks at me suspiciously, the desk clerk raises an eyebrow, the elevator man smiles superpolitely. All I want is lunch, not a three-hour identity crisis." And so, the urban solution, choosing an elite city club and strong-arming the NETWORK lunch club into it, seems less than ideal.

A PLACE IN THE SUN

I am not at all sure that there is an ideal solution for the NETWORK lunch club. In fact, variables from area to area within the United States make pragmatic solutions the most feasible at this time. Basically, all the NETWORK can do is what it *can do* in any particular place, at any particular time. The solution may be a good one for a year or for a decade; we are now in a time of experimenting, and the American virtue of pragmatic solutions, of living one day at a time and muddling through to the next one, is the networks' strength. What the regional NETWORK in New Jersey finally did was totally pragmatic, fortuitous, and probably temporary. We found a nearby restaurant, owned by a woman and adjacent to an expensive apartment complex. The prices are rather high, the location is not terribly convenient, and the portions are too large. But on the credit side, the owner is a woman—a very desirable plus, and one that a NETWORK should seriously consider. The atmosphere is outstanding, because we were lucky enough to meet the owner when she was in the process of renovating a back room for expansion purposes. Our NETWORK took full advantage of this process to suggest changes in the direction of increased daylight, additional privacy, and a lighter tone, all of which make the room perfect as a lunch club setting. Light, air, and a pleasant natural plant-filled decor are all desirable plus factors, which we realized only through experience. The woman-owned restaurant, in the process of renovation, represented an incredible stroke of luck for our NETWORK. If other groups can duplicate this situation and create their own atmosphere for a lunch club, then they will indeed be fortunate.

The mechanics of the lunch club, like the mechanics of the NETWORK directory, turned out to be surprisingly simple. The New Jersey group decided to reserve the room for our own NETWORK use one day per week: we planned to bring business guests there on that day, hold committee meetings, and eat lunch with each other, as well as set aside one day per month for our regular meetings. Every Thursday, from noon to 3 P.M., the room is devoted to NETWORK uses; the room seats about seventy-five people, at tables ranging from two to eight. Some of us can hold committee meetings there while others have business lunches, since neither interferes with the other. In fact, the only time we take over the entire room as a group is on the Thursday when NETWORK has its regular meeting. On the other Thursdays, the room functions much as any private club might: some tables for two are used for client lunches, some tables for four and six are used by NETWORK members dining with each other, and a table of eight is usually reserved for a committee meeting. The comings and goings of the NETWORK members are casual, for relaxation is a goal we have achieved. All that the restaurant owner asked was that we each make reservations in advance for our party. Since we are all business people, that requirement is not arduous: reservations have been made, honored, cancelled with stellar efficiency. We have attempted to schedule business lunches on Thursdays; insofar as we have succeeded, every guest has been pleased with the atmosphere and comforts associated with our lunch club. Even the presence of large numbers of business women has not intimidated or annoyed the male guests. We did achieve our goals of elegance, comfort, ease of dining in a public place. We can meet and relax in an atmosphere of great respectability, and we have achieved recognition, as will be detailed in the next chapter. Relaxation, recognition, and respectability have been achieved by our NETWORK through planning, discussion, and a lot of luck.

FUTUREWORLD

The best possible solution for NETWORK lunch clubs would be the construction and ownership of such clubs: building and operating one's own clubhouse guarantees the kinds of controls that clubs imply. This is an idea of such daring at this point that most NETWORK members gasp: real estate, club management, land and property decisions as well as membership criteria are all a bit mindboggling right now. But it is not all that far-fetched to posit the eventual purchase and ownership of a piece of property for a NETWORK club: If enough affluent career women want this, it can happen. That women have never before combined on this basis to own and operate their own business club is merely indicative of the lack of numbers of women in the position to do so even in the preceding decade. Now, for the first time in modern history, women have access to positions of power which provide them with sufficient funds and knowledge to consider founding their own NETWORK club and buying premises for the purpose. In fact, with enough sharp investors, club property can be combined with rentals, and money can be made on the real estate deal. Imagine the building of a club on a desirable bit of property, as a part of an office or apartment complex: there is money to be made from the rentals, which could provide profit over and above any profit the NETWORK lunch club could make.

Is this visionary? Of course! Even the building of a NETWORK lunch club as a real estate transaction may be futuristic. For the time being, the creation of a lunch club within an existing facility is the priority. But it is not too farsighted to predict the day when these ventures will lead to real estate transactions. Once women have begun to combine in new ways, to organize in a new fashion, to deal with each other on a business and not on a social or reflected status basis, the next step is creating a space for these dealings which represents not the best compromise, but simply the best. The women in networks are gradually amassing the knowledge of professional life, the financial acumen, and the confidence in their own abilities to found groups where mutual interests can be shared. It will be a small step, I think, to *build* clubs that represent a perfect, or close to perfect, blend of circumstances that make re-laxation, respectability, and recognition into a fourth, and crucial, *r: reality!* (Since I wrote this book, at least one club for women has been created, in Toronto, which appears to be analogous to a NETWORK club. To the best of my knowledge, no such club has been formed in the United States—yet!)

Membership

CHAPTER 9

The need for networks to set membership policies represents the most agonizing set of problems women involved in these new alliances have to face. These problems force soul-searching by NETWORK members in ways that they invariably did not count on. Some questions are: Who can be allowed in? Who are the ones who do the allowing? What kind of criteria may be used? Should there even be formal criteria? Is not this whole process redolent of the worst aspects of male clubbiness? Shouldn't women try to set up new modes of togetherness instead of aping outworn fashions dictated by men?

Because these questions are highly charged emotionally, women who set out to form networks often find themselves enmeshed in issues they never wanted to face. This is particularly true of regional networks, which are loosely knit groups without the common bond of the intracorporate or professional women's NETWORK. These are the groups of women who have to face head-on the concepts of elitism, exclusivity, selectivity which are the sum and substance of networking, but which trigger off frightening and ambivalent associations in women's minds.

The basic fears center around a kind of totemic magic possessed by the potent words clustering near the concept of power. It is my contention that women forming networks are already doing so on an elite basis: the necessary mental and verbal justification simply is daughter to the fact. The logic of elite networks is impeccable, and the strongest selling point in favor of exclusivity. If a group is designed to provide peer support, how can it comprise women other than peers? Let us forget all of the male fears that burble up at the sight of women in groups. Networks have only themselves to account to when creating membership policies. In that sense, a NETWORK has to make positive decisions, not settle back into defensive postures. And the most difficult decision to make is the one of exclusivity. This is, however, the most logical one: peer support demands *peers*. Women's groups have concentrated on the word *support* for so long that they have devoted insufficient attention to the idea of peerhood, and the necessary definitions that should follow. It is the idea of peer sharing that must control NETWORK membership if the group is to function usefully.

Women have every right to want to associate with other women on their own level. NETWORK women do, of course, owe a debt to the future, the women behind them on career ladders; there is a moral obligation to set up outreach programs for younger or later-starting women not yet on a high achievement level. Mentoring, on a woman to woman basis, forms the subject of another book; it is a development that will grow out of networking. In the foreseeable future, however, networks should be elite groups, exclusive and selective ones. Executive women need to associate with other professionals on a social and business basis; they do not need to associate with housewives, secretaries, and clericals on the same basis. The future must be distinguished from the present: Networks include groups of women in present power. One of their goals may very well be to assist those destined to take the reins in the next decade, but for now, NETWORK women are perfectly justified in setting up a system of "ins" and "outs." The inexorable law of niceness does not apply when women are setting up peer groups, forming common bonds, and uniting to thrash out career problems. It may not be at all nice to exclude certain women, but the very idea of peer associations carries with it levels of achievement that mandate exclusivity.

Membership policies generate anxiety because the bases for NETWORK exclusivity are so new that women have to invent ways of dealing with their own success. For almost the first time in history, women in sizable, though still very small, numbers are setting up achievement in professional life as a criterion for mutual association. The newness of achievement as a desirable lifestyle as well as the concept of peer in peer support presents the need to create criteria for networks at the same time as the groups are being formed. Superimposed on all of this need for creation is the large amount of publicity generated by NETWORK groups, which immediately leads to women clamoring to be let in. Once the news is out, the group is faced with a membership quandary, before it is even well-defined as a NETWORK group. The New Jersey NETWORK, like most regional groups, had to wrestle with membership policy because we were faced with women who wanted to join after we received a good deal of publicity. We had not, however, formulated any clear ideas about women we wanted to ask. One member said, "We have to decide who the gatecrashers are when the party guest list isn't even made up!" Because the membership quandary faces most networks long before the groups are ready for it, some threads need disentangling in order for the groups to make the right decisions.

DECIDING NOT TO DECIDE

Networking is a conservative activity, a movement, in infancy just now, among women who want to associate with each other beneficially so that each can help the other to move ahead in her career and life as smoothly as possible. Alas, society considers *any* gathering of over two women inflammatory: women, even women of high achievement, are expected to be as invisible as possible. Given the drastic imbalance between male perceptions of women's grouping together as incendiary, and most women's own tendencies to work within the system, a low profile is the better part of valor for networks. Unfortunately, all the publicity surrounding the simultaneous nationwide birth of networks works against stately, measured growth: the founding mothers have less time and less space in which to make critical decisions than did our own founding fathers. My feeling is that when a NETWORK is in doubt about creation of a membership policy, acceptance of new women, or determination of itself as a legal entity, the best move is to call a temporary halt to all movement. The NETWORK has to decide not to decide critical matters all at once and at the same time that it is forming. A great deal of time must be wasted, although the more appropriate word is *expended*, at the beginning if overhasty and ultimately regrettable decisions are not to be made. Slowness, informality, nonstructure are perfectly viable for six months to a year, even longer if need be. The reason is that it is extremely difficult to undo a mess once it has been made. The easier task is to think the project through, to decide not to decide certain things immediately, before making the mess! It is far more sensible for networks to indulge in extended debates about membership criteria than to make premature decisions and then be faced with consequences which may be overwhelming.

One reason networks find so much difficulty in tabling sticky issues, like membership, is that women achievers are very structured, goal-oriented, definitive people. The repetition of discussions on the same issue strikes many of us as inane. One of the members of a suburban NETWORK, a late entrant into the business world, said: "The 'membership issue' reminds me of my twenty years of housework. You get all done, and then you find that you have to begin from scratch each time! Can't we get off this spot?" The spot of decisions about membership is not so easy to leave; the women who become part of the NETWORK group will have an impact on the future of the group. And the women left out will undoubtedly bear ill will towards the members for a long time to come. In the press of making decisions, the kinds of things NETWORK women are quite used to, no one has considered the potential problems that disgruntled nonmembers may give rise to. The heady excitement of a new group of women, all of whom have career achievement in common, has fogged over the question of the determined woman, not yet up there and refused admission to a NETWORK, but ambitious enough herself to take measures to remedy her exclusion. I cannot predict the consequences of these disappointed women at this time, because the networks are too new to demonstrate patterns. But I *can* predict that there will be consequences. Because the future is always in question, the desire of the structured women in networks to appear decisive and come up with clear criteria for everything from membership to finances in three months or less ought to be tempered with a recognition that often slow deliberation is best. Just as marriage should be more difficult to arrange than divorce, membership decisions should be arrived at carefully so that undoing mistakes does not become the major activity of networking in the future.

HELP STAMP OUT NICENESS!

A kind of calculated old fogyism implied in the conservative tendency to postpone decisions until all the facts are gathered, all the weighing and balancing done, helps immensely when the membership decisions have to be made. Once women begin asking to join, and once the NETWORK has given sufficient time to studying the question of criteria, the group has to decide whether it is going to be exclusive or inclusive, elitist or populist, nice or rejecting. the NETWORK is free to hash out the issue of who to include for any reasonable period of time: two months is not reasonable, but neither is two years. After this thinking time, however, the membership decision has to be faced. The reason is simple: If the NETWORK refuses to draw up membership criteria, or other plans of action, for an absurdly long period of time, it will collapse as a group because of inertia. So, as always, a balance has to be struck between torturing a subject to death and taking hasty and regrettable steps to let the subject loose. If the fogy does not eventually move one way or another, he turns into one of the stuffed old men in chairs who serve as window decorations for the more prestigious men's clubs.

The image of the old fogy, always male, always solitary, always crotchety, conjures up as its female counterpart the wicked witch: a nasty old lady, doomed to loneliness and lovelessness. She is being punished, of course, for not having been nice. A major reason that networks have so much difficulty with elite concepts is that elitism and niceness are not compatible. The first ingrained impulse of women is to be nice. Mother always said you had to play with the little girl next door, even if you hated her, because it was not nice to reject anyone. The classic, "How would you feel if no one wanted to play with you," is etched in women's brains. The fact that women suffer, in many cases throughout their lives, from fear of rejection themselves is the triumphant maternal corollary to enforced niceness. Women's mental baggage contains the vague hope that if we are nice to people, they won't hurt us and may even be nice in return, allowing us to pass through life without conflict. And so, when women form networks, they agonize over membership decisions because of the old and probably unacknowledged debts to the "What does it cost to be nice?" ethic. The clinker is, however, that women in business and professional positions know perfectly well that it can cost a great deal to be nice. If the name of the NETWORK game is peer support and mutual help, niceness can undercut the entire group by allowing diffusion of interests and levels of success to take place. Overdosing on niceness can result in networks that become replicas of country club lunch foursomes or the local women's club. And if women in networks want to use power directly, and not bask in the reflected power of their husbands and fathers, then they must avoid indiscriminate opening of membership just because it isn't nice to leave women out. Networking women have to recognize their own ambivalence when it comes to setting up criteria of exclusivity because of the conflict with ingrained ideas of niceness. As a research chemist said to me, "It took a long time for me to understand that the old chestnut about 'nice guys finishing last' applied to women as well. I went through college and graduate school being nice to everyone; it's taken me a decade in business to realize that what counts is performance, not goodwill."

Performance is certainly a firm ground for networks. I urge all groups to close ranks on the basis of elitism. Effective networks ought to be clubby, exclusionary, status-laden groups. If we women do not ourselves declare that we are special, select, important, no one else is going to. There is no reason that women in positions of power and responsibility should feel guilty about denying admission to women who are not their peers. If a NETWORK is to be beneficial to the women in it, the NETWORK must include women who can help each other, who can be of use to each other, whom it pays to know. Regional networks have to form the women's power base in a particular geographical area and openly declare that this is exactly what they are doing. Nothing at all is wrong or evil with the spirit of exclusiveness or the articulation of it; it has made men's clubs, and probably society at large, function throughout the ages. Men have rarely felt conflicts about excluding whomever they felt like on any or no particular grounds at all except that Mr. X "didn't belong." Private clubs have traditionally been so exclusionary to blacks, Jews, Catholics, and women that these clubs' decision, forced or otherwise, to enlarge their membership, makes news. And news is not made by nice guys!

SEXUAL SEGREGATION

Perhaps the strongest strand in the complex of fears about creating exclusive membership policies for networks is that this kind of segregation has historically been the property of men running their clubs and by extension, the world. I think that the tired argument, that women in power must not ape the worst of men's vices, reeks of sexual illogic. Until a better, feminist way of running the world and its economy is found, women have little choice. The current population of two percent of executive talent as female is not the kind of number that will create immediate revolutionary change. The quickest way to successful networking is for women to use the available models. If men have M.B.A.'s, we have to get our own: the M.B.A. is everywoman's power tool. If men cluster into power bases in clubs, we have to form our own. The

NETWORK lunch club may very well turn out to be a transitory stage in the development of peculiarly feminine power modes. Meanwhile, it can serve as a perhaps literal everywoman's club. Too many women of goodwill and determination have been thwarted by the argument, "You don't want to turn into a man, do you?" Examine the argument! The answer is not, "No!" The answer is, "How? How can I do it? How can I carve out my rightful share in a man's world?" Until the better matriarchal way is set up, women have to beware of adjurations that giving up niceness and using male power tactics causes us to grow beards. All it does is give women access to power, without which we cannot even begin the search for better ways to run the world.

It is quite ironic that just as men's clubs are being pressured to desegregate, and women's clubs are also facing similar pressures, networks are wrestling with what appear to be the same problems. But the irony, like the good literary device it is, involves a discrepancy between reality and appearance. Elite networks setting out to establish membership criteria involve the formation of totally new entities, for women that is, which posit exclusivity on a totally new basis. I hesitate to use the word, but a NETWORK is a new kind of women's club *segregated* on a new basis. I think, however, that the word is inaccurate: Exclusivity is not the same thing as segregation, elitism is not synonymous with prejudice, selectivity is not akin to reverse discrimination. Women's networks are springing up which appear to be setting up as criteria for joining all of the things traditional social clubs, both men's and women's have been faulted for: power, money, status, position, education. Women, traditionally the liberals in the fight for others' rights, appear to be setting up their very own systems of segregation.

This dilemma emerged at a midwest regional NETWORK which had to field three problems simultane-

ously in deciding how and where to expand: the desegregation of a previously all-male lunch club to include
women, the desegregation of a local women's club to include blacks and Jews, and the insistence of currently
non-NETWORK women that they be allowed to join what
seemed like a jolly group. The NETWORK was faced with
three membership choices. It could link up with the men's
club: that would provide a convenient lunch premise, but
also create pressure from male member's wives to be let
in. It could meet at the local women's club, also very convenient for lunch, where there would be pressure from the
"ladies" to be allowed into the NETWORK. Or, it could remain on its own, as an elite NETWORK, creating membership criteria as well as a club lunch site on its own. As one
member of the nucleus group of thirty women said, "How
can we do anything right? Here we are exultant over the
men's club's taking in women, and the women's club's
taking in Jews and blacks, and now we are planning to set
up a new little segregated enclave."

SNOBBERY AND SEGREGATION

I think that fears of furthering segregation have to
be put to rest. In defense of the elite spirit of networks, and
their desire to include only those women who have
achieved the required status, there are indeed many
similarities philosophically to men's and women's clubs.
There are also many similarities to Phi Beta Kappa, the
Young Presidents' Club, and American Express Golden
Card holders: All are groups of superachievers, clubs created on specifically elitist principles. There are vast differences between creating a group of high level career
women which excludes women not on that level, and auto-

matically barring people on entirely *other* grounds, such as race, religion, or nationality. The historic bases of male discrimination—race, religion, and ethnic background—simply do not arise when women decide to NETWORK. Neither snobbery nor social segregation takes place on NETWORK membership agendas: the criterion is achievement. Standard snobbism just does not arise in networks because women in business and the professions are so new to the success category, such isolated entrants on the elite scene, that what they have in common, their success as women, is far more visible than any distinctions on other bases. Black women physicians and W.A.S.P. women advertising directors have more in common as successful women than they have separating them as black or white, Baptist or Presbyterian, Tuskegee or Vassar graduates. Women of all races, religions, and ethnic backgrounds draw together if they were similarly situated in terms of career achievement. Women who arrive at the same place, like most pioneers, are not too fussy about where each has come from. For a woman, being there at all, being close enough to success to have problems and dreams that she wants to share with other women, is the badge of visibility.

The true NETWORK support system is needed by achieving women as women; achievement is the only criterion for membership. The reason networks have so difficult a time setting down even the mechanisms for exclusivity is that the old and outworn concepts that governed exclusion would not work even if today's new woman wanted them to. The women who have made it to the top are so few in number that their dominant characteristic is their femaleness. As such, the networks include representatives of all races, creeds, countries of birth: it is probably a good thing that, as one midwesterner said, "We're too raw to worry about breeding and too classless to bother with finicky distinctions between eastern schools and the local cow college. What we have to remember is we're all women!"

THE FRATERNITY OF WOMAN

Networks, then, do not have a history of exclusion of women on the traditionally male-biased grounds of race, religion, ethnicity. Networks, in fact, have no historic membership criteria at all to fall back on: they are in the business of self-creation. Another problem, however, is that the sorority-fraternity spirit haunts most networking women's minds; the sex and sociability syndrome characteristic of high school and college groups lingers on to cloud the issue of inclusion by right of achievement on the nonsexual stage. Since NETWORK structures are not based on race, religion, or family background, perhaps a sexual and social element should be considered as another fogging agent. Once women have been convinced that they have a perfect right to set up exclusive, elite, selective clubs based on career achievement, definitions of *elite* become crucial. And here the elements of the sorority system that linger on have to be swept away, because the networks are attempting wholly new kinds of organization. The previous banding together of women in sororities, and after marriage, in women's clubs, took place on an underlying foundation of reflected sexual and social status.

The three s's of our youth were sorority, sexuality, and socialization. Sororities were places where women of similar backgrounds could group to market a sexual hard-sell: here were gathered large numbers of desirable future mates for the fraternity brothers. Sorority membership implied the Good Housekeeping seal of approval by the other women in this socially select group. Membership announced a degree of social acceptibility as well as sexual availability: sororities were the pool into which fraternity boys dipped at will, eventually to select the right mate. *Not* to join a sorority meant removal of one's inviolate self from the pool of sexual and social availability, a refusal to play the mating game. To women now, anxious about forming networks, the 1950s banners of conformity and the sexual marketplace keep on waving like red flags. Women who want to set up membership criteria for networks almost always say, "Now this is *not* going to be like my old sorority!"

But how do women then justify an elite group? How do we set up membership rules without wearing the old sorority sweater? How do we exclude others without shuddering at mother's injunction, "Be nice!" How do we recover from fears of being rejected as punishment for rejecting others? The answer to all of the above has to be, "with difficulty!" The NETWORK concept of elitism involves totally new structures for women. The kind of power elite creation at which networks aim is so new for women that the rules of the game are being written on an *ad hoc* basis. Women have been out of the male power network for so long that prior to a very few years ago, it would have been almost impossible to set up a NETWORK of influential women lawyers, doctors, business executives, academicians. This kind of group was not possible before the women's movement; even though the interwar years saw larger percentages of career women than the fifties and sixties, these women did not have the permission slip to organize provided by the women's movement. Women in the 1930s who carved out careers did so not only as loners, but also with every expectation of remaining isolated, different, unique. To them, *sister* meant your mother's daughter. Prior to the past decade, there have been no concepts of even failed sisterhood. If the women's studies movement has done nothing else, it has given women a right to a past of their own, albeit a dismal one. The very concept that we are not alone, we are not doomed to weird careerism, we do have ties to other women in space and time forms the philosophy underlying the new consciousness of women.

The networking spirit is a new sense of togetherness, that awful word, a kinship not possible in the decades before women's studies grew up. And so, a NETWORK of women, or even more impressive, simultaneous networks springing up all over the country and grappling with the same demons of elitism in choice of members could not have occurred before the seventies. The problem is a new one because the implicit permission to unite, the mother's note allowing the successful woman not to be the one and only, forms perhaps the major heritage of the sixties women's movement and the seventies women's studies programs.

The NETWORK elitism, then, the justification for women's desires to form an elite on a professional and not a social basis, on direct access to power, not borrowed status, is also brand new. If women are not to band together as sexually and socially elite on the basis of the men they have captured, then clearly they must form an elite on their own merits. And that bottom-line kind of exclusivity is what the networks seem to be aiming at. All over the United States groups of women are saying, "Here are other women we want to rub shoulders with. We all form an elite, and we want to get to know each other better. We want to deal with each other." These networkers are suffering the pangs of guilt about their desire for elite status and elite associations. Just at the time when men's clubs are beginning to reconsider membership criteria and become more inclusive, just at the time when women's social clubs are also being pushed to reconsider old modes of discrimination, along comes a new group of women, bonding together in new ways, setting up new kinds of elite systems. No wonder the women in networks are ambivalent, confused, torn by conflicting impulses, agonizing over necessary decisions about who to let in as members, and who to keep out. Mental health in women has always been measured by our ability to face a kind of cosmic craziness, and overcome it!

COIN OF THE REALM

Because the rules of networking are so new, nearly every group begins with the obvious membership criterion: earned income. One member of a regional NETWORK began the discussion by saying, "Look, why waste time? Let's just set a salary limit. Anyone making under $25,000 a year is ineligible." Although that kind of elitism would be easy—numbers are so delightfully tangible—financial criteria will not work in a regional NETWORK that crosscuts all fields of endeavor. If networks are to include women from varied professions, businesses, academic, political, and artistic worlds, financial status does not form a useful passport to elite status. The woman poet, for instance, probably could not meet any income criteria whatever, yet she belongs in an intellectual elite. The woman lawyer just starting out could also be in a lower income bracket, yet she belongs in an influence elite. The woman politician making a dollar a year, or even a thousand dollars a year, belongs to a power elite; the academician, earning less than the average receptionist, belongs to the prestige elite. So earned income as a criterion for membership is not useful; too many women fall outside the money and power axis because of career choices not tied to high salaries, beginning status as professionals, or, in extremis, career selections that are in effect pro bono work. Yet these very women may form important elements in the womanpower elite in a region. When we consider that one half of one percent of the working women in the United States make over $25,000 a year, we have to be flexible in networks as far as setting up income as a measure of status.

In spite of all of these antimaterialistic arguments, high earned income is a very difficult notion of elitism to eradicate. It is very hard not to measure achievement in dollars and cents; that is the coin of the realm in our society, the American dream with a price tag. Women who *have* made it financially are loath, understandably so, to give up the idea that this badge of achievement may not be the most significant one. Women feel an underlying resentment, which again has to be faced, at other women who can *afford* the luxury of politics or poetry, traditionally lifestyles considered the perks of the wealthy. Those luxuries, public service, devotion to the arts, are almost always made possible because a man is out there, a father or husband behind the woman, earning her daily bread. For the women who have to earn their own bread, and who have done so in the amount of $25,000 and above, there is a strong element of hostility aimed at the women who have not had to. No woman who has ever yearned to take care of herself but been handicapped by the habit of "being taken care of" can fail to understand the concept of financial elitism. Still, for networks to turn away the woman who chose a difficult path, but one which happens to be financially unremunerative, is counterproductive. The elite status conferred by high income has to be tempered by respect for those who have chosen public service or dedication to the arts because they were fortunate enough to possess what used to be labeled *independent means*. Some dedicated, high-achievement, thoroughly successful career women cannot be measured as NETWORK members by bottom-line figures because they are not on that particular scale. Salary as a definition of elite status does not provide the infallible guideline for women in regional networks that one would like it to.

SPONSORS: THE NEW SISTERHOOD

As criteria gradually become eliminated for membership in a NETWORK, the whole matter seems to get more and more amorphous. If we eliminate race, religion, ethnic background as historic tools of segregation; if we eliminate sexual and social desirability as gender-related irrelevancies; if we eliminate earned income as a capitalist-based inaccuracy, how can we possibly define elite? The definition of one of us grows vaguer. But is this necessarily bad? Those of us in networks recognize career commitment, achievement orientation, the success ethic when we see it. Like J.P. Morgan's knowledge that he could afford a yacht when he did not have to ask the price, women in networks know other women in the power elite by subtle means revolving around self-confidence, self-worth, projection of positive images. My New Jersey NETWORK hit on the mechanism of sponsorship by the founding mothers as the sole criterion for membership. In other words, to become one of us, at least two charter members have to sponsor a new member for her to be considered. She must be, according to our rules, a woman of professional status. And we left it at that. We deliberately opted for open-endedness in criteria, to leave future membership open to the discretion of current members. The concept of sponsorship is the easiest way of ensuring the kind of elite we want, without tying the NETWORK into a set of rules that cannot be helpful in an area where nearly every successful woman is an exception to nearly every rule. Networks would do well to rely on the discretion and interest of their nucleus group to determine membership, at least until the numbers of women eligible grow so huge that this mechanism becomes unwieldy. At the current level of women in the managerial ranks, that awesome two percent, in any one area of the country there will not be great hordes of influential, powerful, prestigious women storming the ramparts.

The mechanism of sponsorship is startlingly simple: a membership committee consists of all of the charter members, generally no more than two dozen in the average NETWORK. Two of these charter members must show up at a membership committee meeting to sponsor a new member. As with most groups, a very limited number of women are even interested in attending the membership committee's meetings; we consider ourselves lucky to have five founding mothers in attendance, but are content with only three. We did add to the requirement for "professional status" the following item: "At no time shall the membership be overly concentrated in any one field of endeavor or any one firm." This kind of exclusionary practice is essential in a regional NETWORK to prevent overloading by one profession or one corporation. This caveat is needed to keep the regional base viable. For networks formed on an interdisciplinary base, the crosscurrent of careers should be as varied as possible. The newly forming networks do not want to become extensions of one powerful area corporation or even a local branch of a professional women's group; different careers, different businesses, different influence bases are needed for the cross-fertilization of mutual support and shared input to work out best.

The sponsorship of a new member by two members is a fail-safe to ensure a fairer kind of selection. New Jersey NETWORK wanted to be sure that future members would be acceptable to more than one isolated member, to avoid the ugly kind of dispute that can arise when one member thinks a newcomer is a marvelous addition to the group, and the other members think she is awful. One of our founding mothers brought an associate to a meeting. The new candidate for NETWORK monopolized the entire session, giving the group a game plan for life and constantly making suggestions both intrusive and unwelcome. She was disruptive, and not at all professional in the cool, confident sense that the rest of us value; she tried too hard, was too eager to prove her worth, was too pushy in providing input, and did not listen to what had already been done. Immediately after the luncheon, another founding mother called me and launched into a series of complaints about the proposed member. I agreed, and called the inviter, who pointed to the impressive achievements of her associate. I said that Ms. X was undoubtedly all that she was advertised to be, but that there were obvious personality conflicts involved. It was precisely to avoid this kind of confrontation that our NETWORK later decided on the need for two sponsors. We found that no second charter member would sponsor Ms. X, and so finessed—through sheer luck—a potentially nasty situation.

The new applicant, in addition to needing two sponsors, also must fill out a questionnaire and attend one meeting. The purpose of filling out the questionnaire is obvious: I had declared a moratorium on chasing our members for information to be added to the directory! As far as attending a regular monthly meeting, clearly the purpose was to have the entire membership look over the prospective candidate, and vice versa. The entire regular NETWORK crowd ought to have the opportunity to meet the proposed member, as well as the proposed member's having the chance to meet with the networking women. Although we felt that we were imposing the burden of being on display upon the candidate, in practice this need to attend a monthly meeting has cost our NETWORK as well as others some excellent members. Our NETWORK was spurned by a woman we very much wanted to join, the program director of a huge suburban shopping center, on the grounds that we could do her very little good. NETWORK members must realize that there are as many possible rejections of them, as candidates to be rejected! During the regular meeting, the group and the new member can test out the interactions and decide whether the association will be beneficial.

UNANIMITY: VETO POWER

Even sponsorship by two members did not seem a sufficient guarantee for elite membership, where no written criteria could be assigned. A further means of ensuring that the NETWORK remained composed of women who were one of us had to be the dreaded veto power. We decided upon the need for the unanimous vote of all members of the membership committee present at the membership meeting to accept the new member. In other words, she must be sponsored by two founding mothers and then *not opposed* by any one of the remaining NETWORK original members. The message here is that any member who is so violently opposed to the candidate that she feels the group is endangered must show up to vote against her. For a member to be accepted, she must merely be proposed by two charter members, and then voted in by the others at the membership committee meeting. Since between three and five founding mothers usually attend these meetings, they do indeed control the elite nature of the group. But this is the fairest and easiest way to ensure a smooth and harmonious NETWORK, for only the truly abrasive prospect, the woman who has inspired strong feelings in a current member or who strikes someone as totally unsuitable, will inspire an objecting charter member to show up and cast her veto. In fact, this negative event has not happened. The sponsorship and voting run very smoothly, since in every organization, only a small number of women will care about each issue strongly enough to join committees. Sponsorship takes care of women who ask to be allowed in; we simply announce that women must be sponsored to become members. When asked, sometimes irately, how one gets to be sponsored, we tell the truth. Women on a certain level in most geographical areas get to know each other in a short time. If they are utterly unknown, they must *become* known to NETWORK effectively.

Even in cities, even in New York, the achieving women are known to each other—if only by name—through an interlocking system of alumni groups, professional organizations, political caucuses, and social ties. It sounds as if a tiny world of powerful women exists, and, as a matter of fact, that is the case. Sponsorship by NETWORK members is a rather accurate way of perpetuating the power elite, since the numbers of women in that rarified group are so small. The truest definition of elite as a criterion for membership, the most unerring perception of peerdom, takes place not in the form of salary guidelines or schools attended, but in the recognition of one woman by others as *one of us*. The mechanism of sponsorship of future members by current NETWORK members enables that kind of identification to take place.

The final check is the requirement of unanimity: all the charter members of the NETWORK must approve the new member, even if in absentia. If the new member turns out to be not one of us, the blame falls not on the sponsors, but on the rest of the group who failed—or did not care—to object at the right time. New Jersey NETWORK felt that the cohesiveness of the original group, the harmony, the club spirit, ought to be kept up: if one member judged a future member to be disruptive or negative, in a group as small as fifty the member with strong feelings should be allowed to prevail. The most successful networks are in fact very small: anywhere from thirty to one hundred women in any given region. In a group that small, one or two women who do not fit in, who irritate others, can create very negative fallout. Perhaps if networks had hundreds of members, a few misfits could pass unnoticed. But with networks self-limited in size by virtue of their elitist bent, members who do not fit in find their faults writ large. Thus, our group decided on unanimity for admission. While most of the founding mothers do not bother to attend membership meetings, one nay-sayer can veto the prospective member. Again, it has not yet happened. We hope that it won't. But if one proposed member represents a threat to a viable, harmonious NETWORK, the mechanism for excluding that woman exists.

NO BERTIES YET

The need for membership-defined criteria for membership, an inbred elitism, has a rationale: it is that women achievers in networks are so new that we do not have time to come up with some particularly feminist professional variant on selecting members. We networkers must use the mechanisms left to us by both the patriarchal society and our old attempts to squeeze into it. We use the sorority and men's club veto system because we have not had time to invent new ones. There is no conscious desire to ape patriarchy or to follow feminine modes of sorority selection. Those of us interested in networking simply take the systems at hand and use them, so that we can get on with life and success in it. There is not even much conscious thought about the past systems of group formation; we just fall into patterns. Maybe when the networking movement has had time to slow down and reflect, new systems for ferreting out the elite or even redefining the concept of elite will be invented. Until then, networks will be using the old membership criteria time-honored by fraternities, sororities, and clubs of all sort: control of membership criteria by the few, determination of elite status by those self-designated as possessing it, and above all, perpetuation of networks as groups of women who are one of us. Women will have arrived as forces in the power spectrum when, like the English, we can tolerate the dippy eccentric— Wodehouse's "Bertie"—in our midst. For now, we must lend each other support in the most economical way possible, by networking with those we can identify as fellow elite careerists, able to provide meaningful input to each other.

NEW JERSEY NETWORK MEMBERSHIP CRITERIA

The membership shall consist of women of professional status. At no time shall the membership be overly concentrated in any one field of endeavor, or in any one firm.

Candidates for membership will be sponsored by two members in good standing, will be asked to complete a questionnaire regarding professional or business status, and will have attended at least one monthly meeting.

Candidates meeting the above qualifications for membership will be proposed by their sponsors to the membership committee. Such candidates will become members upon unanimous vote of all members of the membership committee present at the membership meeting, and upon payment of dues.

Reprinted courtesy of the New Jersey Network Membership Committee (criteria procedures).

Publicity and Backlash— The Crisis Phase

CHAPTER TEN

There are three striking facts about NETWORK publicity: (1) it is easier to gain publicity than any NETWORK first imagines; (2)publicity can occur in two areas of the print media: *Lifestyle* sections or *Business* sections; (3) the implications of publicity differ depending on the section in which the original NETWORK stories appear.

Most networks are unaware of these distinctive possibilities; they seek publicity without realizing that perhaps there should be either efforts to *avoid* certain types of media attention or deliberate attempts to place stories where the most beneficial attention can be gained. Stories on the *Lifestyle* page emphasize the NETWORK as a group of women; stories on the *Business* page focus on the NETWORK as a group of *career* women. Accenting *women* puts publicity on the page read most by women; accenting *career* women puts publicity on the page generally read by men. When the publicity appears on the *Lifestyle* page, membership problems arise: women, the readers of that section, want to join the NETWORK group, and the group has to decide membership policy. But when publicity appears in the *Business* section, no automatic respect accorded the NETWORK by the largely male readership will result. Instead, there may be a sharp backlash directed against successful women that can take the form of further, and this time negative, publicity.

So the matter of publicity for a NETWORK is a double-edged sword; it isn't simply a matter of *what* is said, but a complex mingling both of *what* and *where*. Problems arise for the NETWORK no matter where the original stories appear, problems which should be planned for in advance, since they often catch embryonic groups by surprise.

Publicity for NETWORK groups usually is limited to newspapers, magazines, and journals; radio and TV are not yet involved in NETWORK publicity. I suspect that, because of the ease of gaining publicity, all an enterprising publicity chairwoman of a NETWORK has to do is alert a radio or TV station to the network's desire for air time; however, I would caution extreme circumspection in so doing because of possible unforeseen consequences. The wrong kind of exposure can be more harmful to a NETWORK than no exposure at all, especially in the network's formative months. Given the eagerness of the media to pay as much attention to networks as has been the case, I can foresee no problems in gaining publicity, once the decision has been made to do so. Let the decision be a conscious and informed one on the network's part, a planned goal of radio and TV coverage, and the fact will quickly follow the press release!

READ ALL ABOUT IT!

One reason for my confidence in networks ability to reach radio and TV channels is the amazing ease and quantity of publicity networks have already attracted in print. This is a point bearing close examination.

Most groups hold elaborate strategy sessions planning ways to get media attention; there is a whole art to press releases, public relations, getting in the news. Part of this art involves merely gaining attention; the success of the publicity chairperson is often measured by his or her ability to gain any kind of coverage at all. In fact, it is not an oversimplification to point to the entire American industry of advertising and public relations to stress the need felt by organizations for public visibility. Squadrons of highly paid people strive for just that.

Given the American dream of visibility, it took a while for me to notice the apparently disarming ease with which networks received media coverage. There have been articles all over the United States, ranging from the *Wall Street Journal* and *Business Week* to small local newspapers about the *old girl networks* that have been formed. I have a bulging, but by no means complete file of clippings sent to me by women throughout the country about local networks. The news seems to hit the papers and magazines with extraordinary ease. Part of the overwhelming amount of NETWORK news is the loose and confusing use of the word NETWORK; it can refer to any group from specifically communications executives, for the term is originally a communications one, to groups of women getting together in the ways I am discussing. Headlines are deceiving: not every NETWORK story is about a NETWORK as this book defines it. The word is very much in the popular domain, and by no means carries a clear-cut, well-defined meaning. Apart from that, and the tendency of people to read headlines but not much more, it does seem that all that is needed for overdoses of press attention is a declaration by twenty or thirty women that they are meeting to form a NETWORK.

Why do networks make the news so quickly and with so little effort? The P.T.A, the Library Board, even political parties need a good deal more effort to attract media attention. Why is NETWORK activity highlighted? To begin with, NETWORK press releases are generally professional productions by a NETWORK member, even though done on a volunteer basis. Many of us have done our stints as publicity chairwomen in the days when women, who can all magically "write well," either got to be recording secretary, corresponding secretary, or publicity person in every group from the local church auxiliary to the Boy Scouts. Further, because of this connection between women and the craft of writing, one member of most regional networks turns out to be a mover and shaker in the media: Our New Jersey group counts as a member the editor of a *Lifestyle* page, as do groups in Ohio, Florida, and Indiana. Traditionally the media field has been less inhospitable to women than, let us say, the construction industry. Networks quite often have members who are editors or publishers of magazines and newspapers. It is no accident that the *only* female Chief Executive Officer of a Fortune 500 company is Kay Graham: the longest-standing historical connection of women and careers has been in the realm of writing. So the presence of media women in a NETWORK, and the ability of numbers of NETWORK women to write high quality press releases is a constant.

Still, would that it were always as easy to gain publicity as writing a one-page press release which automatically summons photographers, reporters, and front-page positioning! While it doesn't hurt to have a newspaper editor in your NETWORK, or to have many members who can turn out a fascinating press release, neither of these guarantees that an organization's news will make the front pages. Other organizations of businesswomen have had real problems in gaining coverage even for special events like fund-raising dinners, scholarship drives, and charity works. One member of a businesswomen's group told me that they were desperate for media coverage: "We are able to offer outstanding speakers, reasonably priced dinners, a profit that goes to respectable charities—all this to the fourteen women who show up!" The difference between these older semicharitable, semiprofessional groups and networks is that the older groups compete with dozens of other groups for media attention. Networks, on the other hand, are *NEWS*.

NO NEWS IS GOOD NEWS

The NETWORK concept of women organizing for purposes which are totally new is what makes networks highly newsworthy. Women grouping together from many different career areas to support each other on a professional, business basis is such a radical departure from previous organizational efforts of women that this networking becomes news as soon as the item is let out of the meeting room. Women are known to organize easily for causes: from the temperance and abolition movements on, women have been instrumental in organizing for *others'* causes. In their own women's movement, while the ability to organize was not at first doubted, the effectiveness of the group was ultimately open to serious questions. Suddenly, women who had mobilized huge efforts on behalf of civil rights were perceived to be ineffectual in gaining their own civil rights: a group of women could band together to achieve justice for blacks, but could not do so for themselves. E.R.A. has been pending since 1923! Silly as it may appear, any grouping of women for other than social purposes has always achieved an inordinate amount of attention. Throw in the words *power, status,* and *ambition*, and you can see the kind of missile you are hurling into the press room.

Any group of women banding together for purposes of creating a power base, a center of influence, an elite of its own is going to create a big splash; simply using the word *ambition* in connection with women is news. When men, the power elite, see more than one woman in one career spot, they are suspicious, fearful, and madly interested. In fact, men perceive women in multiples when there are really only a very few in sight. Ask the average male executive how many female executives there are; if there is even one, he will see many and answer, "Of course we have a lot of women managers here," automatically using the plural form. If you point out that one woman, who is probably in charge of the clerical department, is neither *women* nor *executives*, the average male vice president will say, vaguely, "Well, there must be some others." Men in business, even in the professions, will perceive one woman as so highly visible that she immediately multiplies before their eyes. As the harbinger of many more women to enter the organization, she represents a threat. The male executive fears a kind of massive social revolution in which all the women in all areas of his life refuse to stay in place, and rise up demanding power and status, demanding to be part of the elite.

Such hidden, but very real, fear of a woman's revolution that will shake the foundations of the social order as we know it makes a NETWORK news—and rather frightening news—to the largely male power world. No matter what is said about the younger generation and adaptive lifestyles, we still live in a rather traditional world in which men fear the acquisition of power by women. And these fears may be justified. No one yet *knows* the results of large-scale, female acquisition of power and influence. No one yet knows the results of successful female networking. The news is in the fact that for the first time, women are daring to combine openly in ways that enable them to say, "I have ambition. I want to be a success, and I plan to use other women to help me. I must get to know the right women, learn to make contacts, and make deals with women who can help me get to the top." The very daring of women getting together, *not* to trap men into marriage, or keep them there, and not to help others, but to catapult themselves into positions where they can choose marriage or nonmarriage as a goal secondary to their own success, is astounding. I have heard men, in unobserved moments, off guard, compare the new networks to their image of "bra burning libbers" that haunted the seventies. That there never were any bra-burners does not matter; the negative image is the one that dominates male minds, and female minds as well. So the ease with which networks gain publicity is a measure of fascination with the achieving woman, watchful interest in her, and fear of what she will do next. Making page one is less a tribute to skilled press releases or editorial contacts than it is a response ot the unknown. If you render the incomprehensive visible, you somehow defuse its ability to do harm. I think that the networks' astonishing ease in gaining publicity is an index of male desire to bring this strange and possibly dangerous group of women out in the open, to see what they are up to.

THE FINE ART OF BENEVOLENT NEGLECT

Because the media reflect male control—Kay Graham is the exception, not the rule—this ease in gaining publicity is not an automatic tribute to a brilliant publicity chairwoman or a *Lifestyle* editor. In fact, when NETWORK publicity appears in the *Business* section, the ambivalent nature of the publicity becomes obvious. Networks could do with less publicity at times, and more benevolent neglect. The desirability of publicity is a factor that must be balanced against the need to formulate policy and make decisions that publicity carries in its wake. Getting the public's attention is easier for networks than for any group I have ever worked with; the media is fascinated by the spectacle of successful women daring to meet and articulate words like *ambition, achievement,* and *aggression.* But this very spectacle carries with it the burden for those women of bearing aloft the banner of success. Networks under public scrutiny cannot afford to stumble, look foolish, or hesitate. The very glare of the spotlight, particularly in the *Business* section, demands a kind of perfection that most early networks simply have not yet had time to achieve. One NETWORK member asked me, "Can't I just be me? Why do I have to watch every word in an interview? Since when did I represent an entire class of humanity, *career women?*" The answer is, unfortunately, that at this time, every woman and every NETWORK is not simply an individualized entity. We are all standard-bearers, and have to remember that what we do reverberates. As a member of a NETWORK, any woman will be judged as a representative of all women and all networks. Is this fair? No. But it does affect the way the publicity game works.

LOW PROFILES

For networks, the major point about publicity is not how to get it, but *when* and *where* to get it. Ideally, the question should be *whether* to seek publicity at all; and ideally the answer should be, "Of course not. Who needs it?" The truest index of power is the need to say nothing about it. Groups from the Mafia to the men's clubs of Fifth Avenue know the value of low profile living: When you really have it, you certainly don't have to flaunt it. Not flaunting it is an excellent idea, since if you do, others will want it—they will want in, they will look at you overly much, they may become jealous enough to encroach on hallowed prerogatives. The recognition that real power is silent, effective, and subtle, is one that most people have not achieved. The one hundred most powerful persons in the United States would probably be unfamiliar names to nearly all. But the *realpolitik* of oligarchy, power in the hands of the silent few women, is too far ahead, too futuristic, for networks to achieve within the foreseeable future. The kind of power grouping that a truly low profile clubbiness implies will be, perhaps, the goal of networks in the next century. For the time being, the immediate low profile has to be a reasoned desire to hold back on publicity until the NETWORK feels ready for the public eye.

Since a NETWORK often cannot make that decision, because it is not in a position to withhold information when publicity comes unbidden, the problems attendant upon turning up on the *Business* pages have to be recognized. When a NETWORK makes business news, this is not an automatic badge of success: in fact, the attraction of unwanted and unsympathetic male attention may turn out to be the most salient result. Networks may have to curb their penchant for publicity rather than make efforts to attract it. Being ignored does not mean being neglected. The other half of the coin, attracting lavish attention, may entail the need to fend off the close scrutiny this attention implies. Close attention to networks does not necessarily give rise to burgeoning male approval. The appearance of a story on the *Business* page may not create an instant, newfound respect for women achievers—quite the reverse, in fact. Women with a high profile are almost always seen as far too visible; as such, the public attention networks attract can trigger off old male fears of adverse behavior in women. The examination of headline words illustrates the kinds of negative connotations that networks in the news give rise to.

OLD GIRL NETWORKS

Almost every story in the *Business* press has used the words *old girl* in connection with networks. And almost every woman in or out of a NETWORK recoils from this term. It is quite repulsive on several grounds. First, the obvious addition of agism to sexism hardly helps; *old* is never a compliment to a woman in America. While the parallel *old boy* term may contain a hint of acceptable cuteness—look at those successful men teaming up just like boys!—*old* under no circumstances conveys anything positive about women. Further, the addition of *girl* piles nastiness upon nastiness. *Girl* is a word that applies to females under the age of fourteen; calling a grown woman a *girl* is an insult. It is a derogatory, deprecating term, with no element of cuteness about it at all. The combination of *old* and *girl* is synergistic: the image is one of seventy-year-old women in puffy sleeves cavorting like infants with a kind of senile spontaneity. Adding this to networks does not exactly create a powerful image; we end up with covens of funny old ladies doing unimaginable things in secret. In no way is *old girl* NETWORK parallel to *old boy* NETWORK as an image in the public mind.

Thus, when references are made to *old girl networks* in any of the media—and somehow that always seems to be in the headlines—the image is counter to the purposes of the networks: serious, career-minded women meeting to pursue advancement for each other and future generations of businesswomen. When the New Jersey

NETWORK finally made the *Business* section of a local newspaper, we were most thankful that the words *old girl* did *not* appear in the headlines. One member said, "I shudder every time my boss calls his secretary a girl; I don't think I could deal at all well with being judged part of an old girls' group if our NETWORK were called that in the papers."

WOMEN RIPPING OFF WOMEN

An even worse effect of publicity in the business press is the implication that the whole process of networking is an insidious technique devised by women to rip off other women. The psychological substratum seems to be the idea that once girls grow up, they prey on other women. Even if *old girl* NETWORK is an innocent structure designed to take advantage of parallel grammatical constructions, the accusation of networking as gimmicky or trendy exploitation is not so innocent. The *Wall Street Journal*, certainly the single most influential business publication in the United States, featured this set of accusations in a front-page article on networks: the key headline words were *Sisterhood*, *Gimmickry*, and *Skeptical*; the implication was that networks involved a clever exploitation of women by other women.[1] With all due respect to the very unclear usage of the word NETWORK, and the kinds of difficulty that can arise when words are not used in the same way by various groups, a very negative kind of reporting resulted. This was a case of publicity in the business press having an extremely unexpected and quite un-

[1] Carol Hymowitz, "*Sisterhood, Inc.* Business is Booming For Those Who Help Women in Business. Workshops in Assertiveness and 'Networking' Grow, But Many are Skeptical. "A Lot of It is Gimmickry,' "*The Wall Street Journal*, CXCIV, No. 44, 8/31/79, p. 1.

pleasant result. Several women in networks called me and pointed out the damage to the groups this negative reporting caused. But as one NETWORK member pointed out, "Most women don't read the *Wall Street Journal* anyway!"

While I reluctantly agree with that assessment, and while I am also aware that the article and the groups of networking women are not really about the same thing, the point is that the *headlines*, the juxtaposition of words with negative connotations around the NETWORK banner, were damaging. Even if the article had come out as favorable to networks, this kind of publicity invariably triggers negative responses in male readers. The reasons are rather complex, but as a general rule of thumb, men do not like success stories where the heroes are women. And networks have to be realistic enough to bear that in mind when publicity is the issue. The patriarchy regards any women who legitimately earns over $100,000 a year as a moral leper, particularly if she is a businesswoman, not a doctor or lawyer. A woman's ability to earn that kind of a salary, and the woman who does is quoted as saying *a man's salary*, invites doubts of her ethical probity as well as her business expertise. If she can be shown to prey on other women, so much the better; the male elite can then say, "I told you so!" Because the concept behind networking is contact-making, using, and knowing other women, it lends itself to implications of exploitive activities. That such implications are inaccurate does not matter for page one news. Women in networks do not seek to exploit each other financially, and most women instrumental in setting up the groups have done so as a volunteer activity. Still, the association of the activity itself with women who make a good deal of money, especially those in helping roles, represents a kind of unwanted glare of the spotlight.

My first reaction to the press flap over *Sisterhood, Inc.* as an evil activity was one of surprise; I could not imagine that the networking concept could hit the front page as an uncontrolled and uncontrollable example of greed. I thought of the hundreds of self-help movements ranging from EST to mind control, transactional analysis to rolfing, mostly male managed, which certainly do try to exploit the public, or at best, aim at making their founders quite rich. I also thought of the shadier branches of the analytical tree, where an analyst can be anyone from a physician to a plumber, since mental therapy is a profession with no clear licensure requirements. Some pseudotherapists prey on women. Apparently the true nature of networks and the legitimacy of women's banding together in this way is destined to gain far less headline space than suspicions of witchery, bitchery, or both. The terms *old girls* and *Sisterhood, Inc.* both indicate that women engaged in helping each other, in creating mutual support systems, and in trying to help future generations of women, may not generate immediate understanding and sympathy.

Why should male disapproval be feared? Ideally it should not. But the business media is largely male-controlled; what gets into business papers and periodicals about women is determined by men. It is the old tale of woman as defined by man, Simone de Beauvoir's eternal *Other*. Even when the definitions attempt to be favorable, attempt to set up the idea of *old girl networks* as positive parallels to *old boy networks*, the fallout is negative. Women resent being labeled *old girls*, and men dislike groups of women teaming up together. When the reportage is unfavorable, when networks are made to appear exploitive, the damage done is multidimensional; the men have their worst suspicions about women confirmed, and the women are turned away from the very media that they should be reading. I predict it will be necessary for women to read the *Wall Street Journal* for at least a half-century before we can make substantial changes in its content.

In terms of publicity in the business press, no news is better than bad news. But it is not always the networks who make that choice. They often have no control over decisions to write a story about them, or the content of the story. There is a natural desire on the part of NETWORK members to crow about their achievements; there is no concomitant assurance that the resultant publicity will turn out to be favorable. Once something appears in print, no matter how biased the reporting, the offended party can do very little short of a libel suit. All impulses to seek publicity, therefore, should be tempered by the realization that the end product may be snide, unfavorable, negative. Once said, hard to unsay: perhaps networks should have antipublicity chairwomen! While a NETWORK cannot, of course, refuse to be made media property, keeping a low profile is the best course for the early stages of networking, since there is absolutely no guarantee that any publicity will be favorable.

FRONT PAGE BLUES

The second unexpected and perhaps unwelcome result of NETWORK publicity has taken place when the groups are written up in the *Lifestyle* sections of the press, those pages or sections, even entire magazines, with primarily female readership. What has resulted here is pressure from women not in the NETWORK to get in. Although this pressure is dealt with in the chapter on membership, some words of caution are in order here. While it may be impossible for a regional NETWORK to maintain a low enough profile to keep out of the media entirely, abundant publicity at the early stages of NETWORK meetings forces the group to make premature decisions about membership. Women who read about this new group often feel free to call up and ask to be invited to a luncheon or a meeting; sometimes, if the date, time, and place of the NETWORK meetings are printed in the story, uninvited guests show up by surprise. This reaction to networks can cause a membership crisis long before the group is ready to survive that issue; nothing disrupts harmony more than having to deal with new additions to a group which itself has not become cohesive.

Because a NETWORK can predict that women will be asking about membership after the first story appears on the *Style* pages of the newspaper, advance action can be taken. The NETWORK spokeswoman should make it clear to the reporter, or state in writing, that membership policy has not been decided upon as yet. The terminology can be that membership criteria are *being debated*, *in committee*, *under discussion*, or something equally vague. This kind of statement is not an indication of indecisiveness; it is an open admission that membership criteria present thorny problems, and that the nucleus NETWORK group is working them out.

When this admission is made openly, the NETWORK group can then tell the women who invariably call and ask to join that no decisions have yet been made on membership. The women's names can be taken, and, after due deliberation in the network's own time frame, membership qualifications can be set up. There is no reason that a newspaper or magazine article should force a NETWORK to make decisions before it is ready to. Policy made under the gun of publicity may turn out to be very regrettable in the future. The best way to deal with this situation, one which has emerged in most regional networks, is to try to make it clear in the publicity item that decisions are in process. If the publicity does not mention that the networks do not yet have firm membership criteria, embarrassing situations can arise. After all, networks do not want to be in the position of being vaguely exclusive or of being forced into admitting women who are not wanted. Announcing that there is no stated membership policy as yet leaves the door open for future decisions on membership, as well as creating the distinct impression that there is going to *be* a membership policy.

At this point, I should mention that one of the oldest gambits for exercising absolute control over membership is the *no rules* strategy. The best way to ensure that members are agreeable to the current clubby set is to avoid as far as possible written rules that can be challenged, with everyone proceeding by a rule of thumb that is informal, highly variable, and deadly. Networks as elitist institutions will probably end up here; but networks in the full glare of the spotlight of publicity cannot afford to say so. Admitting that a NETWORK controls membership by *not* having fixed rules is tantamount to inventing a brilliant new secret weapon and then telling everyone about it. Only those with a low enough profile can operate in this fashion. Networks are too new, too interesting to the media to be able to operate in this kind of atmosphere. What they can say, however, with truth, is that since they are new groups, they have not made membership policy just yet, but plan to as soon as practical. The open admission of a lack of policy at present is a useful adjunct to early publicity, since it prevents other problems from arising later.

Open admission of a lack of clear-cut membership criteria is both an honest and legitimate way of providing answers to women who may someday become welcome members of the NETWORK. This admission also turns into an instrument for networks to use in examining their own structure, to see where and how future members can fit in. Measured growth, careful deliberation, weighing and balancing are expected signs of a new organization that plans to survive beyond infancy. A NETWORK loses nothing if, in public announcements or interviews, a spokeswo-

man says, "We have decided that we cannot make binding decisions about membership right now." Confessing to
current unreadiness to make membership policy is no
crime, though fifty years of *no rules* would probably lead
to legal actions similar to those affecting men's clubs. The
NETWORK should not feel forced by early publicity to make
decisions that have to be thought out carefully for a period
of anywhere from six months to a year: this kind of deliberation inspires respect. And the woman on the receiving
end of this information understands full well the logic of an
unformed group's unwillingness to predetermine future
growth.

SUMMARY

The impact of publicity on networks is variable
enough for it to be considered a debatable goal, not a
totally desirable one. The ease with which publicity is
gained is the first clue to a need for networks to rethink the
whole subject of press releases, news stories, and telephone calls to various media contacts. The first question a
NETWORK needs to ask is *when* to seek publicity. Since it is
relatively simple to attract attention, the group has to decide if it wants to: What is to be gained, what is to be lost,
what is the point? While other groups turn cartwheels to
attract a line in the press, networks represent so new a
type of women's group that the members can be sure that
the press will be ready when they are. In fact, the real
problem seems to be not how to get publicity, or even
when to begin seeking it, but rather how to *avoid*
premature publicity. Early networks do much better
operating quietly than having to face the spotlight too
soon. Insofar as publicity cannot be avoided easily, because it is easier to attract media attention when you do

not want it than to get it when you need it, the NETWORK should try to achieve as sympathetic coverage as possible.

The ramifications of publicity differ markedly depending on where the story appears. If networks gain attention in the business press, the implications are generally unfavorable either directly or by negative associations. Calling a group of women *old girls* undercuts the seriousness of purpose behind networks; *old boys* can afford a measure of cuteness because they possess all the marbles in a game where they long ago made the rules. Further, when the business press goes on to associate networks with exploitive females feeding upon other females, real harm is done. The innuendo that women who group together for mutual benefit exploit either each other or other women caters to the worst male fears in the subconscious den of iniquity: woman as bitch, bad alone, but fatal in combination with other women. While it would appear that a women's group which makes the *Business* page has really accomplished a great deal in being taken seriously, the actual kinds of stories belie that optimistic view. It might be best for networks to try to avoid this kind of coverage altogether, although that goal seems unlikely.

The option of appearing in the *Style* section of a newspaper or in a woman's magazine bears with it the membership problem. Women readers who are curious enough about networks to request admission present the fledgling group with the need to define membership policy before they may be ready to do so. This is not to deny that the questioning women may be assets to the group; they may very well turn out to be resourceful, enterprising, ambitious women. After all, if the women have enough initiative to call up after a news story has been published, they may be quite welcome additions to a NETWORK. The point is, the NETWORK may not be ready to expand at that time, but premature announcement of this group forces membership decisions to be brought up. The only way to deal with this problem is to make clear that membership policies have not been decided yet; and, if possible, the NETWORK should notify the media of that fact. If the publicity cannot include it, then the NETWORK members must tell inquiring women that more time is needed. All in all, the final word on NETWORK publicity, no matter when, where, or how often it appears, is that the group has every right to get its own act together—and to say so—before going on the road!

Conclusion

I think that the future woman is the moneywoman.
For that reason, networks will continue to grow and
flourish. The future of the power of women as theoreticians
will continue to be the academic wing of feminism:
women's studies departments on college campuses in this
country and throughout the world. But these programs
will need continued funding. We are heading into what
appears to be a disastrous economy for educational en-
terprises. I am afraid that women's studies programs will
be wrecked by budget cuts, that old device for doing away
with what society considers dispensable anyhow. If there
is retrenchment, and if feminism is to be kept alive, as it
must to provide seeding for ideas that will sprout in public
consciousness decades or even generations later, the
academic wing of women's studies may have to be kept
alive and growing by money earned or commandeered
by other women. This is a startling and somewhat revolutionary philosophical stance, if for no other reason than its
assuming sufficient womanpower to fund entire pro-

grams. But that may very well be the mandate of the future. Imagine if the world suddenly became too poor to subsidize art, literature, or music! Unlikely, but if the world becomes too poor to subsidize theoretical study in the area of women's concerns, women will have to provide the funds. And networks may very well be the forums for women with power, money, and clout to combine to keep what we collectively regard as a general good alive and well.

The same comments can be made for other organizations, not academic or theoretical, which seek to exert favorable pressure on behalf of women's issues such as E.R.A., reproductive rights, and political goals. Groups such as N.O.W. may also find themselves out of funds; as it is, there is currently a shortage of funding which in practice mandates the kinds of issues N.O.W. and related broad-spectrum groups can become involved with. N.O.W. has virtually had to become a single-issue group focusing on the passage of E.R.A. because of insufficient funding to mount simultaneous attacks on all the injustices in our society. The groups which concentrate on practical issues and programs are just as dependent on funding in the future as the groups which focus on theory. And as the general economy becomes grimmer, it becomes more apparent that women will have to provide the funds as well as the moving spirit for their own causes. Networks can provide arenas for women with power who choose to focus on woman-oriented political or social aims.

It is no secret that the business of America is business; Calvin Coolidge, while perhaps not a role model for the average networker, may very well be the prototype of her boss. The business of women in networks of all types is going to have to be money in the future, short-term as well as long-term, if we are not to begin, *AGAIN*, taking giant strides backwards. It may be up to women to keep alive the flame of learning, to subsidize the scholarly research that seems arcane but that, in its own slow and measured fashion, has begun to give women back their past. It may be up to women to consolidate and to pay for the political, legal, socio-economic rights that have begun to give women their own future. The women who bear the burden of keeping the past an ongoing process of unearthed discoveries and ensuring a future where the right to act on these discoveries exists are today's NETWORK women. We in networks who are not afraid to accept power may find ourselves obligated to use this power for the good of one half of the human race from now on.

Another non-secret is that the other half of the human race, the male half, represents the current power structure. Networking is a strategy that has to incorporate interactions with male peers and supervisors as well as with female. Betty Harragan deals with this topic in *Games Mother Never Taught You;* Jane Trahey, Letty Pogrebin, Rosabeth Moss Kantor all point out the need to network politically within the corporate structure. I certainly agree that networking with both sexes is the key to upward mobility. But I do think that before women can reach out to the entrenched power base, they must form their own power centers. And that is what I think this networking movement is all about. Before women as a group can collectively and in large numbers impact on the male patriarchal business structure, we must gather ourselves together and draw strength from common bonds.

Networks are the wave of the future. They represent power, money, and influence centers where women can combine to effect changes that will benefit all women, in an era when not all women are yet involved in the change process. In an age of transition, at the beginning of an age of social revolution hitherto undreamed of, the women who have chosen to combine in new ways in networks will have the ability to write the script for the future. This is an awesome responsibility for today's professional or executive. But the other choice is loss: loss of the past, loss of the future. We cannot afford to dance backwards; too many times have we taken fearful baby steps ahead, only to return to darkness. We cannot afford to forfeit the future. Today's women in networks have the burden of support not only of the present, but also of the future. And right now, the kind of support that seems most urgently needed is money. Women have to join ranks to raise our earning power, not simply for ourselves, but for those in front of us, and for those behind us. If the wave of the future will be the moneywoman, and I see no way of avoiding that necessity, she will be making her contacts, planning her strategies, setting her goals in today's networks. I predict that networks of achieving, successful, committed women will become the single most powerful force for women in the future of this country.

INDEX

achiever's impulse; 19
agendas, 114
application, sponsors, 185–189
artificial networks, 32
avoiding hotels and motels, 161–162
avoiding negative publicity, 196–197

beginning to NETWORK, 36–53
boardroom use, 62
bonding, instant, 32
boy, old, 2, 31,
budget, 114
business card, 33
business lunch, 153
business manners, 33–34
business talk, 78

career advancement, 43
career choices, 108
careers vs. marriage, 108
castration complex, 90
clothing, 30
clubs, network ownership, 167
club ownership, 167
club prestige, 163
committees, need for, 117
communications loop, 16
confidentiality, 79
contact-making, 34
convenience foods problems, 160
cooperation, 16
coping, 24
corporate day's activities, 104–107
creation of committees, 117
credentials, asserting, 127
credit for leadership, 115–116

daring to ask, 82–84
definition, NETWORK, 17
directors, 114
directory publishing, 119
dual career families, 23, 108, 112
dues, 114

educational outreach, 43, 46
elite impulse, 19
elitism, 26–28, 57, 169, 174–182
exclusion by achievement, 178–184
exclusiveness, 153
executive lunches, 39–40
experimentation, 75
exploratory growth, 75–76

favors, trading, 7
fears:
  of other women, 84
  of arousing male fear, 91
  of male ridicule, 92

of intrusion, 127
first phone call, 40
frequency of meetings, 49–50

game plan, 2
geographic networks, 69
girl, old, 194 201–202
goals, NETWORK, 43
good news, no news is, 196–198
growth problems, 75

honesty, 79

independence, 147
information, trading, 14, 129
instant bonding, 31
interdisciplinary group, 42, 186
interprofessional outreach, 66
invisible women, 5
isolation, 32–37

job seeking, 80
judging other women, 99

kinship group, 30
know, to, 4

lack of membership policy, 207
lady libbers, 150
lawyers, women, 108–109
libbers, lady, 150
lonely lunches, 37–38
lunch, 36–39
lunchtime, 48
location, lunch, 50, 151
low profile, 172, 199–200

male backlash, 94–96
male ridicule, 92–94
manipulation, 10
measuring compatibility, 98
measuring the intangible, 98
media attention, printed, 193–197
membership, 169–191
membership by status, 175
membership by unanimous vote,
  188–190
membership criteria, 173
membership policy, lack of, 207
money, discussion of, 81

need for directory, 120
need for structure, 118
need for titles, 118
negative publicity, avoiding, 196–197
negative reaction, 25–26